ALL TIME

ALL-TEAM

PRO FOOTBALL QUIZ

ALL-TIME ALL-TEAM PRO FOOTBALL QUIZ

JEFF MARCUS

TAYLOR TRADE PUBLISHING
Lanham • Boulder • New York • Toronto • Plymouth, UK

Published by Taylor Trade Publishing
An imprint of Rowman & Littlefield
4501 Forbes Boulevard, Suite 200, Lanham, Maryland 20706
www.rowman.com

10 Thornbury Road, Plymouth PL6 7PP, United Kingdom

Distributed by NATIONAL BOOK NETWORK

British Library Cataloguing in Publication Information Available

Library of Congress Cataloging-in-Publication Data
Marcus, Jeff, 1949–
    All-time, all-team pro football quiz / Jeff Marcus.
       pages cm
    ISBN 978-1-58979-901-1 (pbk. : alk. paper) — ISBN 978-1-58979-902-8
    (electronic) 1. National Football League—Miscellanea. 2. American
    Football League—Miscellanea. 3. Football—Examinations, questions, etc.
    I. Title.
    GV950.5.M37 2014
    796.332′64—dc23
                                                                    2014004542

♾™ The paper used in this publication meets the minimum requirements of
American National Standard for Information Sciences—Permanence of Paper
for Printed Library Materials, ANSI/NISO Z39.48-1992.

Printed in the United States of America

CONTENTS

ACKNOWLEDGMENTS

I am indebted to my agent, and lifelong friend, Anne Marie O'Farrell, without whom this book would not exist. I would also like to thank my editors, Flannery Scott and Karie Simpson, for all of their help.

NFL SECTION

1. What former Pittsburgh and Detroit Lions backfield star later served as a US Supreme Court Justice?

2. Gone Hollywood—Match the former NFL player with his notable movie or TV role:

   1. Jim Brown
   2. Fred Dryer
   3. Rosey Grier
   4. Mike Henry
   5. Alex Karras
   6. Ed Marinaro
   7. Merlin Olsen
   8. O.J. Simpson
   9. Bubba Smith
   10. Woody Strode
   11. Carl Weathers
   12. Fred (the Hammer) Williamson

   a. *Black Caesar* (Tommy Gibbs)
   b. *Blazing Saddles* (Mongo)
   c. *The Dirty Dozen* (Jefferson)
   d. *Father Murphy*
   e. *Hill Street Blues* (Joe Coffey)
   f. *Hunter*
   g. *The Naked Gun* (Nordberg)
   h. *Police Academy* (Hightower)
   i. *Rocky* (Apollo Creed)
   j. *Spartacus* (Draba)
   k. *Tarzan* (three movies 1966–68)
   l. *The Thing with Two Heads* (Jack Moss)

3. Which Hall of Famer, known mainly as a quarterback, holds the NFL record for highest single-season punting average?

4. Who was the first player to surpass 1,000 yards rushing in a season?

5. Los Angeles has been without an NFL team since 1995. Which team began its existence there?

   a. Oakland Raiders
   b. Arizona Cardinals
   c. St. Louis Rams
   d. San Diego Chargers

6. True or False: Gerald Ford was the only US president to play in the NFL?

7. Who has led the NFL in rushing yards for the most seasons?

   a. Jim Brown
   b. Eric Dickerson
   c. Adrian Peterson
   d. O.J. Simpson

8. Match these current NFL teams with their original locations:

1. Chicago Bears	**a.** Boston
2. Detroit Lions	**b.** Dallas
3. Kansas City Chiefs	**c.** Decatur, Illinois
4. Tennesee Titans	**d.** Houston
5. Washington Redskins	**e.** Portsmouth, Ohio

9. When did the NFL and AFL merge?

10. What was the shortest overtime game in NFL playoff history?

11. Match these NFLers with their actual given names:

1. Tiki Barber		**a.** Alvin
2. Bert Bell		**b.** Atiim
3. Bubby Brister		**c.** Bryan
4. Buck Buchanan		**d.** Clyde
5. Red Grange		**e.** DeBennville
6. Fats Henry		**f.** Duane
7. Crazy Legs Hirsch		**g.** Elroy
8. Bill Parcells		**h.** Fred
9. Pete Rozelle		**i.** Harold
10. Bart Starr		**j.** Junious
11. Fuzzy Thurston		**k.** Walter
12. Bulldog Turner		**l.** Wilbur

12. True or False: The Green Bay Packers are the oldest team in the NFL?

13. Of the eight original AFL coaches in 1960 there were two sets of teammates. Who were they?

14. Lee Riley, NFL and AFL defensive back in the 1950s and 1960s, has a well-known brother. Who is he?

a. Ken Riley
b. Mike Riley
c. Pat Riley
d. Steve Riley

15. The Super Bowl is scheduled at a specific city a few years ahead of time and is virtually always played at a neutral site. Prior to the first Super Bowl, was an NFL championship game played in a city other than that of one of the two teams involved?

16. Which team won the 1936 NFL championship?

17. Coaches Jim Harbaugh (San Francisco) and John Harbaugh (Baltimore) faced each other in the Super Bowl in February 2013. Had there ever been brothers who were head coaches in the NFL at the same time prior to this?

18. The success of soccer-style kickers resulted in an influx of foreign-trained players starting in the mid-1960s. Match these placekickers with their country of origin:

1. Morten Andersen	**a.** Argentina
2. Gary Anderson	**b.** Austria
3. Charlie Gogolak	**c.** Cyprus
4. Martin Grammatica	**d.** Czechoslovakia
5. Bobby Howfield	**e.** Denmark
6. Sebastian Janikowski	**f.** England
7. Nick Mike-Mayer	**g.** Germany
8. Horst Muhlmann	**h.** Hungary
9. Mirro Roder	**i.** Italy
10. Jan Stenerud	**j.** Norway
11. Ray Wersching	**k.** Poland
12. Garo Yepremian	**l.** South Africa

19. What former Penn State back played for the Frankford Yellow Jackets (pre-NFL), New York Giants, and Staten Island Stapletons and was a 1923 outfield teammate of Babe Ruth with baseball's Yankees before becoming an on-field game official for the NFL from 1934 to 1954?

a. Hinkey Haines
b. Pat Harder
c. Tommy Hughitt
d. Dean Look

20. Which TV network broadcast the first Super Bowl?

21. Who is the only Heisman Trophy winner to become an NFL head coach?

22. Which NFL coach is the active leader in career victories?

23. Which nine-year NFL veteran running back (1964–72) shocked the sports world by revealing that he was gay a few years after retirement from the league?

24. Who is the 1940 Heisman Trophy tailback from the Michigan Wolverines whose brief NFL career (1946–47 LA Rams) was overshadowed by his decades as a college sportscaster? (Hint: His son starred on *St. Elsewhere* and *NCIS*.)

25. What NFL competitor played for the most teams? (Definition in this case: appeared in at least one game.)

  a. Billy Cundiff
  b. J.T. O'Sullivan
  c. Dave Raymer
  d. Tillie Voss

26. Which immensely popular female celebrity owned the Boston Yanks, an NFL franchise for much of the 1940s?

27. Match these NFL players with the African nation of their birth:

1. Tim Biakabutuka, RB	**a.** Cameroon
2. Ebeneer Ekuban, DE	**b.** Congo (Zaire)
3. Roman Oben, OT	**c.** Ghana
4. Christian Okoye, RB	**d.** Ivory Coast
5. Jerome Pathon, WR	**e.** Nigeria
6. Kato & Wasswa Serwanga, CBs	**f.** Sierra Leone
7. Madieu Williams, S	**g.** South Africa
8. Amos Zereoue, RB	**h.** Uganda

28. True or False: Renaldo Nehemiah, the multiple world record setter in hurdles, played in the NFL.

29. Who was the one-year 49er back who went on to a decades-long career as an NFL back judge, field judge, and replay official?

   a. Royal Cathcart
   b. Dean Look
   c. Ed Marion
   d. Fred Sweringen
   e. Armen Terzian

30. Who was the first black coach in NFL history?

   a. Tony Dungy
   b. Fritz Pollard
   c. Art Shell
   d. Lovie Smith
   e. Mike Tomlin

31. What QB lasted 21 NFL seasons, mainly as a backup, spending time with the 49ers, Steelers, Lions, Giants, Colts, and Dolphins?

32. Which Ole Miss tackle is in both the college and pro halls of fame and played for Brooklyn (1938–44) and New York of the AAFC (1946–47)?

   a. Dick Barwegan
   b. Red Conkright
   c. Ox Emerson
   d. Bruiser Kinard

33. How many teams that won NFL championships are now defunct?

a. 1
b. 2
c. 4
d. 5
e. 8

34. When was the last time an NFL franchise went out of business?

35. Match these NFLers from the Americas with the country where they were born:

1. Junior Gallette, DE	a. Argentina
2. Bill Grammatica, K	b. Barbados
3. Chris Joseph, RB	c. Bermuda
4. Tim Mazzetti, K	d. Brazil
5. Alan Pringle, K	e. Colombia
6. Fuad Reveiz, K	f. Cuba
7. Luis Sharpe, T	g. Haiti
8. Rocky Thompson, RB	h. Honduras
9. Renaldo Turnbull, LB and DE	i. Jamaica
10. Steve Van Buren, RB	j. Mexico
11. Floyd Wedderburn, OT	k. Venezuela
12. Luis Zendejas, K	l. Virgin Islands

36. True or False: QB Roman Gabriel was the first overall selection in both the NFL and AFL drafts in 1962.

37. What scholarship brought placekicking great Jan Stenerud to Montana State from his native Norway in the early 1960s?

a. academic
b. football
c. hockey
d. ski jumping
e. soccer

38. Which NFL player wrote the scathing *Out of Their League* bestseller detailing the violence, racism, and drug abuse in the league soon after retiring from pro football?

    a. Ronnie Knox
    b. Joe Don Looney
    c. Dave Meggyesy
    d. Chip Oliver
    e. Duane Thomas

39. Which one of these early Super Bowl announcers was not an NFL player?

    a. Tom Brookshier
    b. Paul Christman
    c. Al DeRogatis
    d. Curt Gowdy
    e. Kyle Rote

40. In the NFL's early years there have been several 0–0 ties. When was the last scoreless NFL contest?

    a. 1923
    b. 1930
    c. 1943
    d. 1951
    e. 1977

41. Super Bowl XLVII losing coach Jim Harbaugh (SF) was a former NFL QB. Who is the last Super Bowl–winning coach to play in the league?

42. Match these NFL players with the Pacific Rim country where they were born:

1. Eugene Amano, C	a. Korea
2. David Dixon, G	b. Marshall Islands (Kwajalein)
3. John Jackson, OT	c. Okinawa (Japan)
4. Todd Lyght, CB	d. New Zealand
5. Vai Sikahema, KR and PR	e. Philippines
6. Jack Thompson, QB	f. Samoa
7. Hines Ward, WR	g. Tonga

43. What season saw the first NFL championship game?

a. 1920
b. 1921
c. 1925
d. 1932
e. 1933

44. True or False: The NFL once made a full selection of draft choices for a team that wasn't in the league yet?

45. Who was the first president of the league when it started in 1920 (as the American Professional Football Association)?

a. Bert Bell
b. Joe Carr
c. George Halas
d. Carl Storck
e. Jim Thorpe

46. When was the last time an NFL team left to join a rival league?

a. 1926
b. 1937
c. 1941
d. 1946
e. 1960

47. Which one of these Hall of Fame stars did *not* do double duty as his team's punter or kicker?

    a. Sammy Baugh
    b. Paddy Driscoll
    c. Don Hutson
    d. Gale Sayers
    e. Jim Thorpe

48. True or False: Baseball Hall of Fame great Jackie Robinson played in the NFL.

49. What Basketball Hall of Fame coach (Loyola–Chicago, 1925–42) was an NFL end for the league's first seven seasons (1920–26) and was player-coach of Louisville in 1926?

    a. Otto Graham
    b. George Halas
    c. Lenny Sachs
    d. Tillie Voss

50. Match these past NFL players with their relative:

1. Tim Berra, WR	**a.** Baseball Hall of Fame catcher
2. Dave Butz, DL	**b.** Heavyweight boxing champion
3. Cris Carter, WR	**c.** Hall of Fame QB
4. Anthony Dorsett, S	**d.** Hall of Fame running back
5. Brian Griese, QB	**e.** NBA basketball player and coach
6. Eddie Murray, K	**f.** NHL hockey all-star
7. Ken Norton, LB	**g.** Olympic gold medal winner
8. Rodney Peete, QB	**h.** Nixon administration cabinet member
9. Bobby Taylor, CB	**i.** PGA golfer

NFL ANSWERS

1. Byron "Whizzer" White. White's NFL career was with Pittsburgh in 1938 and the Lions in 1940–41.
2. 1. c; 2. f; 3. l; 4. k; 5. b; 6. e; 7. d; 8. g; 9. h; 10. j; 11. i; 12. a.
3. Sammy Baugh, Washington, who averaged 51.4 yards per punt in 1940.
4. Beattie Feathers, Bears rookie, in 1934. (That milestone was not achieved again until Steve Van Buren of the Eagles did it in 1947. Feathers, incidentally, never came close to that mark again.)
5. d. The Chargers played in Los Angeles in 1960, the AFL's first season, before moving to San Diego in 1961. (Oakland began in Oakland, played as the LA Raiders from 1982 to 1994, then returned to Oakland. The Cardinals began in Chicago and had a 28-year run in St. Louis before moving to Phoenix. The Rams played in Cleveland before moving to Los Angeles, then on to St. Louis.)
6. False. However, Ford was an All-American center from Michigan who played for the College All-Stars in the annual charity game versus the Chicago Bears in 1935. He didn't go into pro football, but one of his first jobs was as a high school football coach.
7. a. Brown, Cleveland fullback, led the NFL in that category eight times in a nine-year stretch from 1957 to 1965 (finishing fourth in 1962). No other runner has more than four rushing titles.
8. 1. c; 2. e; 3. b; 4. d; 5. a. (The Bears began their existence as the Decatur Staleys. Detroit had previously been the Portsmouth Spartans. Kansas City had been the Dallas Texans in the early years of the AFL. Tennessee was the Houston Oilers. Washington started as the Boston Braves.)
9. In 1966 (June) the merger was announced. The first Super Bowl was played in January 1967 after that season and a common college draft was held, but the AFL continued as a separate entity through the 1969 season.

10. On January 8, 2012, Broncos quarterback Tim Tebow connected with receiver Demaryius Thomas for an 80-yard touchdown versus Pittsburgh only 11 seconds into overtime to win the game.

11. 1. b; 2. e; 3. k; 4. j; 5. i; 6. l; 7. g; 8. f; 9. a; 10. c (actually Bryan Bartlett Starr); 11. h; 12. d.

12. False. The Arizona Cardinals are the oldest team in football, having their inception in Chicago in 1899 (as an amateur squad). They and the Chicago Bears (who had originally represented Decatur, Illinois) are the only original teams left from the NFL's first season in 1920 (when it was called the American Professional Football Association). Green Bay, whose team formation dates back to 1919, joined the league in its second year, 1921.

13. Lou Saban, Boston Patriots, and Lou Rymkus, Houston Oilers, had been teammates on Cleveland in the AAFC, while Sammy Baugh, New York Titans, and Frank Filchock, Denver, were both QBs with Washington.

14. c. NBA player, coach, and executive Pat Riley is Lee's younger brother.

15. Yes. In 1936, the Boston Redskins were slated to host the game against Green Bay. Because of poor attendance in Boston, Redskins owner George Preston Marshall moved the game to New York's Polo Grounds. Marshall moved the Skins to Washington the next season, where they've been ever since.

16. Green Bay prevailed 21–6 over the Boston Redskins.

17. Yes. Ed "Dutch" Sternaman was Chicago Bears co-coach (along with George Halas) in 1923, while Joey Sternaman coached the Duluth Kelleys that year. The Bears and Duluth never played each other that year. Joey had played for the Bears with his brother the previous season and rejoined them in 1924.

18. 1. e; 2. l; 3. h; 4. a; 5. f; 6. k; 7. i; 8. g; 9. d; 10. j; 11. b; 12. c.

19. a.

20. Both CBS and NBC. Because of contracts with the two leagues, each network aired the same game with separate

announcers. CBS had the NFL rights, while NBC had the AFL contract during the season.

21. Steve Spurrier, former Redskins coach and current South Carolina coach.

22. Bill Belichick of the Patriots. He has 187 regular season wins, and 205 including the postseason prior to 2013.

23. Dave Kopay.

24. Tommy Harmon, father of actor Mark Harmon.

25. d. Voss actually appeared in games for Buffalo, Dayton, Chicago Bears, New York Giants, two separate Detroit franchises, the Green Bay Packers, Toledo, Akron, and Rock Island, between 1921 and 1929. That's ten teams—although some historians say 11, considering the 1921 Buffalo All-Americans and the 1929 Buffalo Bisons different franchises. (Although Buffalo suspended operations for a season in 1928, the NFL considered the 1929 team a returning franchise.) Voss also played pro basketball in the ABL in the late 1920s. The ABL was an early major league with teams in cities in the Northeast and Midwest that went out of business during the Depression (before returning in a much more limited scope in the 1930s). QB O'Sullivan and kickers Cundiff and Raymer have all been on 11 NFL squads, but each has only been on the practice squads of several of those teams without seeing any game action.

26. Kate Smith, the singer known for "God Bless America," among many other hits.

27. 1. b; 2. c; 3. a; 4. e; 5. g; 6. h; 7. f; 8. d.

28. True. Known as Skeets, he was a wide receiver with San Francisco from 1982 to 1984.

29. a. Cathcart played for San Francisco in 1950, joining older brother Sam, who was in his second year with the club. Sam Cathcart also played in 1952 and became coach of their alma mater, UC–Santa Barbara, from 1956 to 1974.

30. b. Pollard was Akron Pros co-coach (with Elgie Tobin) way back in 1921. He's in both the College and Pro Football Halls of Fame.

31. Earl Morrall (1956–76).

32. d.

33. d. The five are Akron Pros (1920), Canton Bulldogs (1922–23), Cleveland Bulldogs (1924—with many of the same players as the previous year's Canton), Frankford Yellow Jackets (1926), and Providence Steam Rollers (1928).

34. 1952. The Dallas Texans, a one-year team, were such a dismal failure on the field and at the box office that the league canceled its franchise.

35. 1. g; 2. a; 3. b; 4. d; 5. k; 6. e; 7. f; 8. c; 9. i; 10. h; 11. l; 12. j.

36. False. The Houston Oilers picked him first in the AFL draft, but the late Ernie Davis was selected first in the NFL by Washington. The LA Rams used their first-round choice to pick Gabriel, number two overall. He signed with the Rams.

37. d.

38. c. Meggyesy eventually became Western Regional Director of the NFL Players Association for a time.

39. d. Gowdy did play varsity basketball for the University of Wyoming before embarking upon his broadcasting career.

40. c. The New York Giants and home team Detroit Lions both failed to score on November 7, 1943.

41. Sean Payton of the Saints in Super Bowl XLIV. His NFL career consisted of one game with Chicago in 1987. (The last one with extensive NFL playing experience was Tony Dungy in Super Bowl XLI.)

42. 1. e; 2. d; 3. c; 4. b; 5. g; 6. f; 7. a. (Note: Earlier sources listed Ward's birthplace as Georgia or South Carolina. His mother is Korean.)

43. d. The Bears defeated the Portsmouth Spartans (now Detroit Lions) 9–0 at the indoor Chicago Stadium to win the NFL championship. It was indoors because of several days of snowstorms. The game was necessary because of a tie in winning percentage. The NFL didn't go to regular championship games until the next year, 1933, after it went to divisions for the first time.

44. True. The league selected players in every round of the 1937 NFL draft for a team it didn't have as yet. (The NFL draft first started in 1936.) The Cleveland Rams, a team from AFL II in 1936, were admitted some weeks later. The

first-round draft pick, Johnny Drake, a running back from Purdue, played with the Rams from 1937 to 1941.

45. e. The founding owners who were present at the original meeting elected Thorpe because of name recognition, not because of any particular administrative skill. Joe Carr of Columbus was the new president from 1921 until his death in 1939.

46. d. Owner Dan Topping took his Brooklyn franchise out of the NFL to join the new AAFC in 1946. The club had temporarily merged with the Boston Yanks for the 1945 season because of manpower shortages due to many players enlisting in the armed forces during World War II. Meanwhile Topping bought the NY Yankees baseball team and moved his football team to Yankee Stadium, changing their name to the New York Yankees as well. The AAFC had a different Brooklyn team, owned by baseball's Branch Rickey.

47. d.

48. False. However, Robinson was an All-American back at UCLA and did play a couple of season with Los Angeles of the minor-league Pacific Coast Football League while still playing baseball in the Negro Leagues. Many considered Robinson's talent to be of NFL quality. The league hadn't had any players of color for over a decade (due to an unwritten agreement among team owners). Incidentally, Jackie's college teammate Kenny Washington was among the handful of blacks to reintegrate the NFL in 1946.

49. c.

50. 1. a: son of Yogi Berra, all-time Yankee great; 2. h: nephew of Secretary of Agriculture Earl Butz; 3. e: brother of Butch Carter, former Toronto Raptors coach and NBA guard; 4. d: son of Tony Dorsett, Cowboys; 5. c: son of Bob Griese, Dolphins; 6. f: cousin of Mike Rogers, former NHL star; 7. b: son of Ken Norton Sr., WBC champ in 1978; 8. i: cousin of golfer Calvin Peete; 9. g: son of Robert Taylor, who won a gold and a silver for the 1972 US Olympic track team.

ARIZONA CARDINALS

1. When were the Cardinals formed?

2. When did the Cardinals leave Chicago, and when did they move to Arizona?

3. Did Coach Bruce Arians have NFL head coaching experience prior to joining Arizona?

4. Which member of the Cards' Super Bowl XLIII squad played in the Australian Football League before his NFL career?

5. When is the last time the Cardinals won the NFL championship?
   a. 1966
   b. 1957
   c. 1947
   d. 1943
   e. 1925

6. When is the first time the Cards were NFL champions?

a. 1945
b. 1937
c. 1931
d. 1925
e. 1920

7. How long has the Bidwill family owned the team?

8. Who was the franchise's first coach in the league (in 1920)?

   a. Jimmy Conzelman
   b. Paddy Driscoll
   c. Chris O'Brien
   d. Ernie Nevers
   e. Marston "Marshall" Smith

9. What Cardinal holds the NFL record for most points scored in a single game?

   a. John David Crow
   b. Larry Fitzgerald
   c. Ollie Matson
   d. Ernie Nevers
   e. Neil Rackers

10. Match these Cardinal Hall of Famers with their college:

    1. Charlie Bidwell   a. Georgia
    2. Guy Chamberlin   b. Loyola–Chicago
    3. Jimmy Conzelman   c. Michigan
    4. Dan Dierdorf   d. Nebraska
    5. Walt Kiesling   e. Northwestern Louisiana State
    6. Dick "Night Train"   f. St. Thomas (MN)
       Lane
    7. Ollie Matson   g. San Francisco
    8. Ernie Nevers   h. Scottsbluff Junior College
    9. Jackie Smith   i. Stanford
    10. Charlie Trippi   j. Washington (MO)

11. Who was Arizona's quarterback in Super Bowl XLIII?

    a. Kevin Kolb

    b. Neil Lomax

    c. Matt Leinart

    d. John Skelton

    e. Kurt Warner

12. True or False: No Super Bowl has ever been played in Arizona.

13. What is the actual first name of longtime St. Louis Cards receiver Sonny Randle?

    a. Aloysius

    b. Carmine

    c. Elvin

    d. Ruprecht

    e. Ulmo

14. Who scored two touchdowns for the Cards in Super Bowl XLIII?

    a. Anquan Boldin

    b. Steve Breaston

    c. Larry Fitzgerald

    d. Edgerrin James

    e. Ben Patrick

15. What is the longest tenure of any Cardinals head coach throughout the franchise's long history?

    a. 5 seasons

    b. 6

    c. 9

    d. 13

    e. 21

16. Which Chicago Cards player-coach (1923–24) started his NFL career playing under the assumed name of McMahon and left the team to become the head coach at his alma mater, Harvard (1926–30)?

   a. Eddie Casey
   b. Arnie Horween
   c. Ralph Horween
   d. Dick King
   e. Red Steele

17. Name the recent Arizona tackle whose father was an NBA forward from 1976 to 1986.

18. How many field goals did Neil Rackers kick to set an NFL record in 2005?

   a. 28
   b. 37
   c. 40
   d. 42
   e. 57

19. What 1991 Cardinals number one draft pick never played college football?

20. Where was longtime St. Louis Cards kicker Neil O'Donoghue born?

   a. Alabama
   b. Buffalo
   c. Ireland
   d. St. Louis
   e. Tampa

21. Who coached the Cardinals during their first year in Phoenix (as well as their last year in St. Louis)?

a. Joe Bugel
b. Don Coryell
c. Jim Hanifan
d. Buddy Ryan
e. Gene Stallings

22. Who holds the Cards' franchise record for receiving yards in a game?

a. David Boston
b. Larry Fitzgerald
c. Mel Gray
d. Roy Green
e. Sonny Randle

23. Sportscaster Ahmad Rashad played receiver in the NFL from 1972 to 1982, including his first two seasons with the Cardinals. He changed his name to Rashad in 1973. What was his original name, which he played under as a 1972 rookie in St. Louis?

a. Walker Gillette
b. Gary Hammond
c. Freddie Hyatt
d. Bobby Moore
e. Bob Wicks

24. What Cardinals guard from Boise State was born in Alaska?

25. The Chicago Cards were the visitors in the NFL's first night game on November 3, 1929. Where did they play?

a. Buffalo
b. Dayton
c. Minneapolis
d. Providence

26. What Hall of Fame safety spent his entire career with the franchise—from his playing days in St. Louis to his 30 years as director of scouting and personnel, head coach, GM, and team vice president?

27. Who was the interim co-coach in late 1961 whose résumé included jobs as a CFL player/assistant coach, college assistant, NFL assistant (with the Cardinals, Washington, and the LA Raiders), coach at the University of California, Arena League coach, and NFL Europe coach in a 40-plus-year football career?

28. Name the Cardinals coach who was the son-in-law of Hall of Fame coach Weeb Ewbank, the man for whom he played as a Washington University (MO) undergrad?

    a. Bob Hollway
    b. Pop Ivy
    c. Wally Lemm
    d. Buddy Parker
    e. Charley Winner

29. True or False: Arizona coach Vince Tobin (1996–2000) and former Bears and Indianapolis GM Bill Tobin are brothers.

30. What Chicago Cardinals 1932 coach was a Notre Dame back and a 1931 assistant coach there and was killed at age 38 during the 1945 US invasion of Iwo Jima?

    a. Bull Andrews
    b. Jack Chevigny
    c. Phil Handler
    d. Stump Mitchell
    e. Paul Schissler

ARIZONA CARDINALS ANSWERS

1. The Cardinals are the oldest team in American pro football, having their inception in Chicago in 1899 (as an amateur squad). They are one of only two original teams left from the NFL's first season in 1920 (when it was called the American Professional Football Association). (The other team is the Chicago Bears [who had originally represented Decatur, Illinois].)

2. They moved to St. Louis in 1960 because of dwindling attendance and their status as the second NFL club in Chicago, dwarfed by the Bears' popularity. They moved to Arizona in 1988. They were known as Phoenix for the first several seasons.

3. Yes. He was the acting head coach of Indianapolis for 12 games in 2012 during Chuck Pagano's cancer treatment and recovery period. The Colts went 9–3 during that stretch. Arians was voted the 2012 NFL Coach of the Year, the only interim coach to ever win that award.

4. Punter Ben Graham. Graham, a Melbourne, Australia, native, also played in the NFL with the Jets, Saints, and Lions.

5. c. 1947. The Chicago Cardinals beat the Eagles 28–21 for their second NFL title.

6. d. 1925. The Chicago Cards won the league crown with a record of 11–2–1. There were no playoffs in those days. The Pottsville (PA) Maroons, who went 10–2, disputed the championship, claiming two of the Cardinals' victories came after the NFL's agreed-upon ending date. The NFL voted that the Cards were the champions. Pottsville, which hasn't had an NFL franchise since 1928, still disputes the fact that they aren't considered the 1925 NFL champs.

7. The Bidwell family has owned the team for over 80 years. Charles Bidwell Sr. bought the team in 1933 from Dr. David Jones, a dentist. Bidwell, who was a minority owner of the Bears, bought the team for $50,000. He died in 1947 prior to the season, missing the opportunity to see his team win its first championship in 22 years.

8. b. Driscoll, a back, kicker, and punter from Northwestern University in nearby Evanston, was the team's player-coach

through 1922, then continued to play for the club until 1925. He was sold to the Bears in 1926. (O'Brien was the original owner of the team, while Smith had been the coach from 1917 to 1919, prior to the league's formation.)

9. d. Hall of Fame fullback and kicker Nevers was a one-man wrecking crew on November 28, 1929, in a Thanksgiving game against the Bears. He scored all 40 points for his team with six TDs and four extra points in the 40–6 victory. It's one the NFL's longest-standing records.

10. 1. b; 2. d; 3. j; 4. c; 5. f; 6. h; 7. g; 8. i; 9. e; 10. a

11. e. Warner, who had played in two previous Super Bowls with the Rams.

12. False. Super Bowl XLII took place at University of Phoenix Stadium on February 3, 2008. The Giants beat New England 17–14.

13. e.

14. c. Fitzgerald caught two TD passes from Kurt Warner during the game.

15. b. No coach has accumulated more than six years at the helm. Recent coach Ken Whisenhunt was there from 2007 to 2012. Jim Hanifan piloted them in St. Louis from 1980 to 1985, and Jimmy Conzelman had two three-year stretches from 1940 to 1942 and again from 1946 to 1948 in Chicago.

16. b. Horween and his brother Ralph both used the alias of McMahon while playing with Chicago.

17. L.J. Shelton. His father is Lonnie Shelton.

18. c.

19. Defensive end Eric Swann was drafted based upon his minor league football achievements. He had dropped out of Wake Tech Community College (NC), a two-year school that doesn't field a football team. Swann played in the Pro Bowl in 1995 and 1996.

20. c. He was born in Dublin in 1953. He played his collegiate football at Auburn and played for the Bills and Buccaneers prior to coming to St. Louis. He is the most recent NFL player who was born on the Emerald Isle.

21. e.

22. e. Randle racked up 256 yards on 16 catches for St. Louis against the New York Giants in a loss.
23. d.
24. Daryn Colledge.
25. d. They played against the Rhode Island capital's Steam Roller team, which competed in the NFL from 1925 to 1931.
26. Larry Wilson, who was drafted by the newly moved St. Louis club and stayed employed by the club for 44 years before retiring.
27. Ray Willsey, who was interim co-coach with Chuck Drulis and Ray Prochaska for two games (both wins) after Pop Ivy resigned in December 1961. The two games constituted his only NFL head coaching experience.
28. e. Winner was an assistant under Ewbank, then Don Shula at Baltimore before gaining the Cardinals head coach's job in 1966.
29. True.
30. b. Chevigny resigned from the Cards to take the college coaching job at St. Edwards in Texas for 1933.

ATLANTA FALCONS

1. Which Falcon was the first QB to surpass 1,000 yards rushing in an NFL season?

2. What Atlanta player was the 2008 Associated Press Rookie of the Year (offense)?

3. Who is the father of Rich McKay, Falcons team president (and former GM)?

4. Who did the Falcons select with the number one pick in the 1966 NFL college draft?
  a. Steve Bartkowski, QB
  b. Randy Johnson, QB
  c. Tommy Nobis, LB
  d. Nick Rassas, S
  e. Ken Reaves, CB

5. Who became the Falcons head coach when they joined the NFL in 1966?

a. Leeman Bennett
b. Marion Campbell
c. Norb Hecker
d. Dan Henning
e. Norm Van Brocklin

6. In what season did Atlanta achieve a playoff berth for the first time?

    a. 1969
    b. 1972
    c. 1976
    d. 1980
    e. 1982

7. What coach led the team to their first division title?

8. Who was the first Atlanta running back to get over 1,000 yards rushing in a season?

    a. Jamal Anderson
    b. Warrick Dunn
    c. Dave Hampton
    d. Gerald Riggs
    e. Michael Turner

9. Which two Atlanta backs each accumulated over 1,000 yards in the 2006 season?

    a. Deandra Cobb
    b. Warrick Dunn
    c. Jerious Norwood
    d. Michael Turner
    e. Michael Vick

10. Atlanta's all-time scoring leader is also the NFL player with the most career points. Who is he?

11. Who is the two-time Super Bowl champion, British-born defensive end from the Giants whom Atlanta inked as a 2013 free agent?

12. What Falcons receiver played in the Pro Bowl in four consecutive years from 1990 through 1993?

13. Is former Atlanta great DE Claude Humphreys in the Hall of Fame?

14. True or False: Will Svitek, Falcons tackle who played at Stanford, was born in California.

15. What brought former defensive tackle Bill Goldberg (1992–94) more acclaim than his NFL career?

16. Who was the Falcons' starting QB in their first NFL game in Atlanta on September 11, 1966?

17. True or False: No Falcon has ever led the NFL in scoring.

18. Name the Falcon runner who led the NFC in rushing in consecutive years.

19. Where was former Atlanta DT Travis Hall born?
   a. Alabama
   b. Alaska
   c. Georgia
   d. South Carolina
   e. Wisconsin

20. Who is the Atlanta pass catcher who had at least 100 receptions in back-to-back seasons?

21. True or False: Bobby Petrino was Atlanta's head coach immediately prior to Mike Smith.

22. Did Atlanta GM Thomas Dimitroff ever play pro football?

23. What was owner Arthur Blank's background before buying the Falcons?

24. In 1980 two Falcons were co-winners of the NFL Defensive Rookie of the Year award. Who were they?

25. Who coached the Falcons to their only NFC championship game victory in January 1999?

   a. Jerry Glanville
   b. June Jones
   c. Jim Mora Sr.
   d. Dan Reeves
   e. Mike Smith

26. What Atlanta coach from 1994 to 1996 was a former Falcons QB and later coached the Chargers, the University of Hawaii, and SMU?

   a. Jerry Glanville
   b. June Jones
   c. Jim Mora Sr.
   d. Dan Reeves
   e. Mike Smith

27. What Falcons linebacker was the number one overall draft choice in 1988 but is regarded as a bust because he never lived up to expectations, spending most of his career as a substitute?

28. Which Falcons 1973–74 QB was known as the "General" during his stay with the team?

29. Which cornerback did the Falcons pick in the first round of the 2013 draft? (Hint: His two older brothers are already cornerbacks in the NFL.)

30. What Falcons longtime linebacker and five-time Pro Bowl participant was originally signed as a free agent, not having been drafted by a NFL team?

ATLANTA FALCONS ANWERS

1. Michael Vick ran for 1,039 yards in the 2006 season.
2. Matt Ryan, QB, the Falcons' first draft pick (third overall) that year.
3. The late John McKay, former Tampa Bay Buccaneers coach and College Hall of Fame coach of USC.
4. c. Nobis was a middle linebacker from the University of Texas who played his entire 11-year NFL career for Atlanta. (Johnson was the last pick in the first round, Rassas came in the second round, and Reaves in the fourth. Bartkowski didn't arrive until he was the first overall pick in the 1975 draft.)
5. c. Hecker was a Green Bay assistant coach under Vince Lombardi for eight years before being hired to be Atlanta's initial coach. The expansion club had a dismal 4–26 record under Hecker in two and a half years until he was fired in midseason in 1968 and replaced by Van Brocklin.
6. d. They finally made the playoffs in 1980 in the franchise's 15th year of competition. They won their division with a 12–4 record then lost 12–5 to Dallas in their first-ever playoff game.
7. Leeman Bennett was their coach in 1980. He had been their coach since 1977.
8. c. Hampton had 1,002 yards in 1975. He had passed the 1,000-yard plateau during the last game of the 1972 season

but was then thrown for a loss to leave him a few yards short that year.

9. b and e. Dunn led the team with 1,140 yards, and Vick had 1,039.

10. Morten Andersen, who holds the club mark with 806 in eight years with Atlanta. He has 2,544 points during his 25-year career.

11. Osi Umenyiora, born in London, England.

12. Andre Rison.

13. True. Humphrey was finally elected to the Hall of Fame in 2014.

14. False. Svitek was born in Prague, Czechoslovakia, now the capital of the Czech Republic.

15. He became the WCW and WWE heavyweight wrestling champion after his NFL days and was known simply as Goldberg. He is also an occasional actor and a commentator for mixed martial arts.

16. Rookie Randy Johnson was under center in the franchise's opening 19–14 loss to the LA Rams. Johnson passed for one TD and ran for the second TD himself.

17. True, but kicker Jay Feely led the NFC with 138 points in 2002, six points behind NFL leader Priest Holmes.

18. Michael Turner had 1,371 yards in 2010 and 1,340 yards in 2011.

19. b. Hall, a Falcon from 1995 to 2004, hails from remote Kenai, Alaska.

20. Roddy White, who had a team record 115 catches in 2010 and an even 100 in 2011. He fell short with 92 receptions in 2012.

21. False. Petrino resigned with three games left in the season in 2007 to accept a college coaching position for 2008. Assistant coach Emmitt Thomas became the interim head coach for those three games.

22. No, but his dad, the late Tom Dimitroff Sr., was a QB for Ottawa (CFL) from 1957 to 1958 and an original AFL player with the 1960 Boston Patriots.

23. Blank was cofounder and CEO of Home Depot prior to purchasing the Falcons in 2002.

24. Buddy Curry and Al Richardson, both linebackers.
25. d. Reeves got the team into Super Bowl XXXIII with its win over Minnesota. He was selected as the 1998 AP NFL Coach of the Year that season.
26. b. Jones is still coaching SMU.
27. Andray Bruce. He spent four years with Atlanta and another three with the Raiders.
28. Bob Lee. The nickname was a play on the Confederate Army's head, Robert E. Lee, although the footballer's middle name was Melville.
29. Desmond Trufant from the University of Washington. His brothers are Marcus Trufant (Seattle) and Isaiah Trufant (New York Jets).
30. Jessie Tuggle.

BALTIMORE RAVENS

1. Which quarterback started the Baltimore Ravens' first game on September 1, 1996, leading them to a 19–14 victory over Oakland?

    a. Tony Banks
    b. Kyle Boller
    c. Trent Dilfer
    d. Vinny Testaverde
    e. Eric Zeier

2. Who was the first head coach of the Ravens?

    a. Bill Belichick
    b. Brian Billick
    c. Ted Marchibroda
    d. Ozzie Newsome

3. Who was the Ravens' first ever draft choice in 1996?

    a. Peter Boulware, DE
    b. Ray Lewis, LB
    c. Jonathan Ogden, OT
    d. Duane Starks, CB

4. Were the Ravens an NFL expansion team in 1996?

5. Was current head coach John Harbaugh ever an NFL player?

6. True or False: Linebacker Ray Lewis is the last Raven to win NFL Defensive Player of the Year.

7. True or False: Safety Ed Reed has spent his entire NFL career with the Ravens.

8. Which Raven was not a Baltimore first-round draft pick?

    a. Joe Flacco
    b. Michael Oher
    c. Ray Rice
    d. Terrell Suggs

9. John Harbaugh coached the Ravens in Super Bowl XLVII against his brother, Jim Harbaugh, San Francisco coach. It was the first time brothers faced each other as head coaches in a Super Bowl. Had they ever gone head-to-head previously in the NFL?

10. Which running back led the Ravens in yards rushing during their 2000 championship season?

    a. Obafemi Ayanbadejo
    b. Chuck Evans
    c. Sam Gash
    d. Priest Holmes
    e. Jamal Lewis

11. Who is the only Raven to appear in both of the team's Super Bowl triumphs?

12. Who was the Ravens' starting quarterback in 2001 when they were defending champs?

    a. Tony Banks
    b. Kyle Boller
    c. Randall Cunningham
    d. Trent Dilfer
    e. Elvis Grbac

13. Qadry Ismail was a wide receiver on the Ravens Super Bowl XXXV champions and is now a Ravens radio and TV announcer. Who had the longer NFL career, he or his older brother, Rocket Ismail?

14. Where did Brian Billick coach before taking the Ravens head coaching job in 1999?

15. How many assistants from Billick's Super Bowl XXXV staff were later hired as NFL head coaches?

    a. 0
    b. 1
    c. 3
    d. 4
    e. 6

16. Which Baltimore lineman was the subject of the recent movie *The Blind Side?*

17. What Ravens linebacker advocates legalization of gay marriage and gained notoriety after news that Maryland State Delegate Emmett Burns wrote to Baltimore owner Steve Biscotti asking him to suppress the player's public viewpoint in September 2012?

18. What Ravens center from 2009–12 is a Harvard graduate?

19. How many Ravens (through 2012) come from nearby University of Maryland?

    a. 2
    b. 5
    c. 9
    d. 18
    e. 30

20. Explain the derivation of the team's name.

21. How many Hall of Fame inductees have played for the Ravens thus far?

    a. 1
    b. 2
    c. 3
    d. 4
    e. 8

22. The Ravens' GM is also in the Hall of Fame. Who is he?

23. Match each of these Ravens with his alma mater:

1. Peter Boulware	**a.** Arizona State
2. Joe Flacco	**b.** Delaware
3. Jacoby Jones	**c.** Florida State
4. Ray Lewis	**d.** Lane College
5. Jonathan Ogden	**e.** Miami
6. Michael Oher	**f.** Mississippi
7. Ray Rice	**g.** Rutgers
8. Terrell Suggs	**h.** UCLA

24. What Ravens director of player development and former linebacker for the team is stricken with ALS (Lou Gehrig's disease)?

25. How many years was the city of Baltimore without NFL football between the time the Colts left for Indianapolis and the Ravens came?

26. Where did Brian Billick play college football, and what position did he play?

27. Who did Baltimore pick with the last first-round choice in the 2013 NFL draft?

28. What 2013 linebacker/defensive lineman Ravens free-agent signee previously spent seven years with Denver?

29. Which Raven has started the most consecutive games in team history?

   a. Jarret Johnson
   b. Ray Lewis
   c. Jonathan Ogden
   d. Ray Rice

30. Which one of these future NFL head coaches was *not* a Ravens assistant in their original (1996) season?

   a. Marvin Lewis
   b. Eric Mangini
   c. Mike Nolan
   d. Jim Schwartz

BALTIMORE RAVENS ANSWERS

1. d. Testaverde came to Baltimore with the Cleveland Browns when Art Modell moved his team for the 1996 campaign.
2. c. Marchibroda had previously coached the Baltimore Colts several years before. (Belichick was the last coach of the original Browns, but was fired before the team moved.)

3. c. Ogden was the first, although Ray Lewis, who was still with the team in 2012, was also taken in the first round by the Ravens that year.

4. No. The franchise was the Cleveland Browns prior to moving to Baltimore. (In a deal arranged by the NFL, the Art Modell–owned club could not keep its Browns history or records, which were reserved for the new Cleveland Browns, who began play in 1999.)

5. No. But his brother Jim Harbaugh, now San Francisco's coach, was a Ravens quarterback in 1998.

6. False. Terrell Suggs (LB) won the award in 2011. Lewis won in both 2000 and 2003.

7. False. Reed, Baltimore's first draft pick in 2002, has spent 11 years shoring up the Ravens' secondary but signed as a free agent with the Texans in 2013. Ed Reed also played for the Jets in 2013.

8. c. Star running back Rice was the team's second-round choice out of Rutgers in 2008. The Ravens used their first pick on quarterback Flacco that year.

9. Yes. Baltimore beat San Francisco in a regular season match-up during the 2011 season, 16–6.

10. e. Rookie Lewis led the club's ground game with 1,364 yards.

11. Ray Lewis. Lewis earlier had announced he was retiring at the end of Baltimore's playoff run and went out a big winner with his second Super Bowl ring.

12. e. Grbac was with the KC Chiefs the year before. Cunningham, the backup, started two games while Grbac was injured. Neither of the QBs from their 2000 champ squad, Trent Dilfer or Tony Banks, was retained the next year.

13. Qadry. Both brothers started in the NFL in 1993. Qadry played until 2002 (ten years) while Rocket last played in 2001. A third brother, Sulaiman, played in the Arena League with the NY Dragons but never in the NFL.

14. He had been an assistant coach with Minnesota from 1992 to 1998, the last five years as offensive coordinator.

15. d. Marvin Lewis, Jack Del Rio, Mike Smith, and Rex Ryan all became NFL head coaches, although none was hired in that capacity the next season (2001).

16. Tackle Michael Oher.

17. Brendon Ayanbadejo, who is married to a woman and the father of two children.

18. Matt Birk, who retired a few weeks after the Super Bowl XLVII victory.

19. b. They are WRs Torrey Smith and Jermaine Lewis, CBs Josh Wilson and Dominique Foxworth, and T Jared Gaither.

20. The name comes from Edgar Allan Poe's most famous poem, "The Raven." Poe lived most of his adult life in Baltimore and is buried there.

21. d. Jonathan Ogden, the franchise's original draft pick, is the latest to gain enshrinement, in 2013. He joins Deion Sanders, Shannon Sharpe, and Rod Woodson, all of whom primarily played for other teams.

22. Ozzie Newsome.

23. 1. c; 2. b; 3. d; 4. e; 5. h; 6. f; 7. g; 8. a.

24. O.J. Brigance.

25. 12 years. The city wasn't devoid of pro football during that entire period—the Baltimore Stars won the USFL championship in 1985 after moving from Philadelphia, and the Baltimore Stallions were members of the Canadian Football League in 1994–95. They won the 1995 Grey Cup CFL championship but moved to Montreal the next season, 1996, after it was announced that Baltimore was getting NFL football again.

26. He was a tight end for BYU in the late 1970s.

27. Matt Elam, a safety from the University of Florida.

28. Elvis Dumervil.

29. a. Johnson, a linebacker from 2003 to 2011, started a team-record 129 straight games. The streak ended when he moved to the Chargers for 2012.

30. c. Nolan was an assistant with the Ravens, but not in their first year.

BUFFALO BILLS

1. Buster Ramsey was the Bills' first coach when they played in the AFL's first season, 1960. What was his coaching background just prior to joining Buffalo?

    a. coach of the University of Buffalo
    b. assistant coach for the Chicago Cardinals
    c. coach of Canisius College
    d. assistant coach for the Detroit Lions
    e. coach of William & Mary

2. What Bills quarterback from their early AFL days later became an Upstate New York congressman and was the vice presidential candidate on the Republican ticket with Bob Dole in 1996?

3. Name the Bill who was the first runner in AFL history to top the 1,000-yard mark for a season:

    a. Wray Carlton
    b. Elbert Dubenion
    c. Cookie Gilchrist
    d. Terry Miller
    e. O.J. Simpson

4. In what year did O.J. Simpson become the first player to rush for over 2,000 yards in an NFL season?

   a. 1969
   b. 1971
   c. 1972
   d. 1973
   e. 1975

5. When was the last time the Bills won a league championship?

   a. 1963
   b. 1964
   c. 1974
   d. 1990
   e. 1993

6. Which coach has won the most games during the Bills' existence (including the AFL years)?

7. What kicker missed a last-second field goal attempt that would have beaten the New York Giants in Super Bowl XXV?

   a. Steve Christie
   b. Pete Gogolak
   c. John Leypoldt
   d. Rian Lindell
   e. Scott Norwood

8. When is the last time Buffalo made the playoffs?

9. Which Buffalo QB has the team record for most touchdown passes in a career, in a season, and in a game?

10. Which Bills QB has the team record for the most passing yards in a season?

   a. Drew Bledsoe
   b. Joe Ferguson
   c. Ryan Fitzpatrick
   d. Jim Kelly
   e. Jack Kemp

11. Match the Bill with his given first name:

   1. Butch Byrd   a. Carlton
   2. Chan Gailey   b. Charles
   3. Cookie Gilchrist   c. Fulton
   4. Flip Johnson   d. Garrard
   5. Buster Ramsey   e. George
   6. O.J. Simpson   f. Orenthal
   7. Bubba Thornton   g. Thomas

12. Who has owned the Bills franchise from its inception in 1960 through the current time?

13. Which 1986 Lombardi Award linebacker from the Alabama Crimson Tide was obtained by the Bills in a trade with Indianapolis after he was a contract holdout until midseason 1987?

14. True or False: There was a previous NFL team called the Buffalo Bills.

15. What player did the Bills select with the first overall NFL draft pick in 1985?

16. Who is LB Jay Foreman's father?

17. Which Bills running back led the AFC in rushing yardage in 1990, 1991, and 1993?

18. Which QB did the Bills make the first passer picked in the 2013 NFL draft?

    a. Matt Barkley, USC
    b. E.J. Manuel, Florida State
    c. Ryan Nassib, Syracuse
    d. Geno Smith, West Virginia

19. Who holds the NFL record for longest field goal in a Super Bowl?

20. Name the two Bills who won the Heisman Trophy.

21. What Bills guard and six-time Pro Bowl participant was elected to the Hall of Fame in 2003?

22. Who coached the Bills and later attained Hall of Fame status for his playing career as a center?

23. Which Bill is the only player in AFL history to score more than one safety in a season?

    a. Butch Byrd
    b. Richie McCabe
    c. Ron McDole
    d. Marty Schottenheimer
    e. Tom Sestak

24. How old was the Bills' oldest player in the first AFL season, 1960?

25. Where was Leif Larsen, Buffalo lineman from 2000 to 2002, born?

a. Austria
b. Germany
c. Luxembourg
d. Norway
e. Sweden

26. True or False: Coach Doug Marrone is a former Bills player.

27. Who is the longtime Bills interior lineman who won the Outland Trophy in 1979, had his number retired by NC State, and is in the College Football Hall of Fame?

28. Which original Bill won the 1959 Maxwell Award while at Penn State and played QB, HB, DB, and returned kicks during the team's first two seasons (1960–61)?

a. Stew Barber
b. Roger Kochman
c. Richie Lucas
d. Tom Sherman
e. Tom Urbanik

29. Prior to the Bills, when did Buffalo first have an NFL franchise?

30. How many Bills QBs made at least 25 passing attempts in 1960, the first AFL season?

a. 1
b. 2
c. 3
d. 4
e. 5

BUFFALO BILLS ANSWERS

1. d. Ramsey was a Detroit assistant for eight years before being hired by the Bills. He had played at William & Mary and spent his six-year NFL career as a guard with the Chicago Cardinals.
2. Jack Kemp.
3. c. Gilchrist ran for 1,099 yards for the Bills in 1962, the AFL's third season. He had previously played in the Canadian Football League and was signed before that season.
4. d. O.J. totaled 2,003 yards rushing in 1973. He accomplished this in a 14-game season for a new (at the time) NFL record.
5. b. The Bills won their second straight AFL championship in 1964, defeating San Diego for the second year in a row.
6. Marv Levy, Hall of Fame inductee, has 123 wins. Lou Saban is a distant second, with 70 victories.
7. e. Norwood missed wide right on a 47-yard attempt that would have given the Bills their first NFL championship. The Giants hung on 20–19 in one of the closest Super Bowls ever. Buffalo is still looking for its first NFL title.
8. They earned a wild card spot in 1999.
9. Jim Kelly. The Hall of Famer has 237 lifetime TDs, and had 33 in the 1991 season and connected for six TD passes on September 8, 1991.
10. a. Bledsoe had 4,359 yards passing in 2002.
11. 1. e; 2. g (actually Thomas Chandler Gailey); 3. a; 4. c; 5. d; 6. f; 7. b. (Thornton was a Buffalo receiver in 1969–70 and has been a celebrated track coach at the University of Texas for several decades.)
12. Ralph Wilson Jr. Wilson started the team as an original AFL franchise for 1960 and has owned the team ever since. He was elected to the Pro Football Hall of Fame in 2009. Wilson died on March 25, 2014.
13. Cornelius Bennett.
14. False. A team of the same name played in the All-America Football Conference from 1947 to 1949. (They were called the Bisons in 1946.) They applied for NFL membership in 1950 during the NFL-AAFC merger but were rejected

while the league admitted Baltimore, Cleveland, and San Francisco to its ranks.

15. Defensive end Bruce Smith. The choice proved to be a good one—Smith played 15 seasons for Buffalo and was inducted into the Pro Football Hall of Fame in 2009.

16. Chuck Foreman, star running back for the Minnesota Vikings in the 1970s.

17. Thurman Thomas. Thomas had his best total in 1992 (1,487), when he didn't lead the conference.

18. b. Manuel was the only QB taken in the first round in 2013.

19. Steve Christie. His 54-yarder set the all-time mark versus Dallas in Super Bowl XXVIII and was the first field goal of at least 50 yards in the history of the big game. There have been three of 50 or more yards since.

20. O.J. Simpson and Doug Flutie.

21. Joe DeLamielleure.

22. Jim Ringo, the great center of the Packers' 1960s dynasty, coached the Bills for a year and a half, mid-1976 and all of 1977. Ringo relieved Lou Saban, who resigned after five games in 1976.

23. c. McDole had two safeties in 1964.

24. Thirty years old. Opening day starting QB Tommy O'Connell, a former Bear and Brown, was 29 when the season opened but turned 30 late in September. Every other player was in his twenties that first year.

25. d. He's from Oslo, Norway's capital city.

26. False. Marrone did play in the league as an offensive lineman for two years, but it was for New Orleans and Miami.

27. Jim Ritcher, who played for Buffalo from 1980 to 1993.

28. c.

29. In the first season, 1920, when it was known as the APFA, the Buffalo All-Americans were a leading contender. That franchise played until 1929 (skipping the 1928 season). It changed its name to the Bisons, the Rangers, and back to the Bisons before going out of business.

30. d. Rookie Johnny Green led the club with 228 passes, Tommy O'Connell had 145, Richie Lucas had 49, and Bob Brodhead had 25.

CAROLINA PANTHERS

1. In what year did the Panthers first compete in the NFL?

    a. 1987
    b. 1993
    c. 1995
    d. 1996
    e. 1999

2. Who was Carolina's starting quarterback in their expansion season?

    a. Steve Beuerlein
    b. Kerry Collins
    c. Jake Delhomme
    d. Cam Newton
    e. Chris Weinke

3. In what city does Carolina play its home games?

    a. Asheville, NC
    b. Carolina, PR
    c. Charlotte, NC
    d. Charleston, SC
    e. Raleigh-Durham, NC

4. What job did Dom Capers hold prior to becoming the Panthers' first coach?

5. What distinction separates owner-founder Jerry Richardson from all of the other NFL owners?

   a. He once was the Governor of South Carolina
   b. He also owns an NHL hockey team, the Carolina Hurricanes
   c. He's a neurosurgeon
   d. He's a former NASA astronaut
   e. He played in the NFL

6. True or False: Current head coach Ron Rivera played in the NFL?

7. What Panthers' second-round draft pick QB in 2010 had a disappointing showing that season, leading to the drafting of Cam Newton the very next year?

   a. Derek Anderson
   b. Hunter Caldwell
   c. Jimmy Clausen
   d. Matt Moore

8. When was the first time Carolina got to the NFL playoffs?

   a. 1995
   b. 1996
   c. 1999
   d. 2000
   e. 2007

9. What is Cam Newton's full first name?

    a. Camelot
    b. Cameron
    c. Camilo
    d. Campbell
    e. Camus

10. Who holds the Panthers record for career sacks?

11. What player has scored the most points in Carolina history?

    a. John Kasay
    b. Muhsin Muhammad
    c. Steve Smith
    d. Wesley Walls
    e. DeAngelo Williams

12. Who holds the Carolina team record for most receptions in a career, season, and single game, and most receiving yards in a career, season, and single game?

13. Who was the blond, long-haired linebacker who made the Pro Bowl in two of his three years with the Panthers before retiring?

14. Which coach has the worst single-season record in team history?

    a. Dom Capers
    b. John Fox
    c. Ron Rivera
    d. George Seifert

15. Match the recent Panther with his alma mater:

1. Jon Beason   a. Auburn
2. Jake Delhomme   b. Boston College
3. Ryan Kalil   c. Louisiana–Lafayette
4. Luke Kuechly   d. Memphis
5. Olindo Mare   e. Miami
6. Captain Munnerlyn   f. Navy
7. Cam Newton   g. South Carolina
8. Steve Smith   h. Syracuse
9. Mike Wahle   i. USC
10. DeAngelo Williams   j. Utah

16. What is Tim Biakabutuka's actual first name?

    a. Taymond
    b. Thomas
    c. Timothy
    d. Timson
    e. Tshimanga

17. Where did 2012 NFL Defensive Rookie of the Year Luke Kuechly (LB) play his college ball?

18. True or False: Jason Peter, defensive end from 1998 to 2001, has a brother in the NFL.

19. Cam Newton broke the franchise record for passing yardage in his second career game. Which QB's record did he break?

    a. Steve Beuerlein
    b. Kerry Collins
    c. Jake Delhomme
    d. Chris Weinke

20. What Panthers career rushing leader was shot and killed by his wife after a domestic dispute during the summer in 2000?

21. Which of these Panthers stars didn't play his entire NFL career with the team?

   a. Jon Beason, LB
   b. Jordan Gross, T
   c. Kris Jenkins, DT
   d. Dan Morgan, LB
   e. Mike Rucker, DE

22. True or False: No player who suited up for the Panthers is in the Pro Football Hall of Fame.

23. What tight end made the Pro Bowl squad in five of his seven years with Carolina?

24. Who is the first Panther to surpass the 1,000-yard rushing mark?

   a. Michael Bates
   b. Tim Biakabutuka
   c. Anthony Johnson
   d. Fred Lane

25. True or False: Carolina had two 1,000-plus yard receivers in 1999.

26. Who was the original GM for the Panthers?

   a. Dave Gettleman
   b. Marty Hurney
   c. Mike McCormack
   d. Jerry Richardson
   e. George Seifert

27. True or False: Ryan Kalil's brother is also an NFL center.

28. Name the Panthers number one draft choice in 2004 who is the career interceptions leader and played with the team until 2012?

29. True or False: 2013 first-round draft choice Star Lotulelei (Utah, DT) was born in American Samoa?

30. What job does former safety Mike Minter (1997–2006) currently hold?

    a. astronaut
    b. college football coach
    c. North Carolina state legislator
    d. TV host

CAROLINA PANTHERS ANSWERS

1. c.
2. b. Collins was the franchise's first draft pick, fifth overall in 1995.
3. c. The team plays in Charlotte, the largest city in either of the Carolinas.
4. In 1994, Capers was the defensive coordinator of the Pittsburgh Steelers under head coach Bill Cowher.
5. e. Richardson is unique among current NFL owners in the fact that he actually played in the league. He was a backup flankerback (wide receiver) for the Baltimore Colts from 1959 to 1960, including the 1959 championship squad. He was the Colts' 13th-round draft choice out of little Wofford College in Spartansburg, South Carolina, in 1958.
6. True. Rivera was an NFL linebacker with the Chicago Bears from 1984 to 1992. He was their second draft pick in 1984. He was a sub for Chicago's Super Bowl XX club, becoming a starter a few years later.
7. c. Clausen remains a backup on the team, though he hasn't played a down since 2010.

8. a. The Panthers got all the way to the NFC final in 1996 before losing 30–13 to Green Bay. They had won their division with a sparkling 12–4 record in only their second year of competition.

9. b. Cameron Jerrell Newton was drafted as the first overall pick by the Panthers in the 2011 NFL Draft. The former Heisman Trophy winner from Auburn University won the 2011 NFL Rookie of the Year award.

10. Defensive end Julius Peppers accumulated 81 sacks for Carolina from 2002 to 2009.

11. a. Kasay, the Panthers' placekicker from 1995 to 2010, had 1,482 points for the team record.

12. Steve Smith. Smith has 772 career receptions, 103 catches to lead the NFL in 2005, with 14 coming on November 20 of that year. He has 11,452 receiving yards with a high of 1,563 in 2005 (NFL league leader) and 201 in the October 30, 2005, game.

13. Kevin Greene, Hall of Fame candidate who played on Carolina in 1996 and again in 1998–99.

14. d. Seifert led the team to a horrendous one-win, 15-loss 2001 campaign. The team's only win came on opening day. Seifert was fired soon after and hasn't coached since. That year was in sharp contrast to his glory days as the San Francisco 49ers' coach, where he won two Super Bowls.

15. 1. e; 2. c; 3. i; 4. b; 5. h; 6. g; 7. a; 8. j; 9. f; 10. d

16. e.

17. Kuechly is a three-year star from Boston College who declared early for the NFL draft and was the Panthers' first selection in 2012 (ninth overall). He hails from Cincinnati.

18. True. Christian Peter was an NFL defensive tackle from 1997 to 2002 for the Giants, Colts, and Bears.

19. d. Weinke, the backup QB starting for the first time in five years because of an injury to Delhomme, threw for 423 yards on December 10, 2006. He was the oldest Heisman Trophy winner for FSU at 28 years old before coming to Carolina as a rookie.

20. Fred Lane was a talented but troubled Panther back from 1997 to 1999, traded to the Colts in the off-season in 2000, before his life was cut short at age 24.

21. c. Carolina traded Jenkins to the Jets for two draft picks in 2008, and he spent his final four seasons there. (Note: Jon Beason also left Carolina during the 2013 season, joining the NY Giants.)

22. False. The late defensive end Reggie White, known primarily for his years in Philadelphia and Green Bay, unretired at age 38 after a year out of the NFL to play one season for the Panthers in 2000. He was posthumously elected to the hall in 2006.

23. Wesley Walls.

24. c. Johnson had 1,120 yards on the ground in 1996, the team's second year of competition.

25. True. Muhsin Muhammid led the club with 1,253 yards, and Patrick Jeffers had 1,082.

26. c. McCormack was hired as the team's first GM and club president in 1993, almost two years before the team began play. He had previously been Seattle's GM and had been the head coach of Philadelphia, the Baltimore Colts, and Seattle prior to his employment with Carolina. He was an offensive tackle in the league in 1951 for the defunct NY Yankees, served military duty during the Korean War, missing the 1952 and 1953 seasons, and was an anchor on the Cleveland Browns line from 1954 to 1962. He was inducted into the Pro Football Hall of Fame in 1984 as a player.

27. False. His brother Matt is a tackle for Minnesota.

28. Cornerback Chris Gamble.

29. False. He is a native of the island nation of Tonga.

30. b. He was hired as head coach of little Campbell University (NC) for 2013.

CHICAGO BEARS

1. What Bears' 1961 NFL Rookie of the Year was Coach of the Year for the club in both 1985 and 1988?

2. Which defensive end led the NFL with 17 sacks in 1985 for the champion Bears?
   a. Richard Dent
   b. Dan Hampton
   c. Al Harris
   d. Mike Hartenstine
   e. William Perry

3. Which Bear was Pro Bowl MVP three years out of four?

4. True or False: Ten-year Bears RB Matt Suhey is a third-generation NFL player.

5. Dick Butkus replaced another future Hall of Famer at starting middle linebacker for Chicago. Who was the aging star who became a sub in 1965?

a. Doug Buffone
b. Joe Fortunato
c. Bill George
d. Rudy Kuechenberg
e. Larry Morris

6. Which two Bears running backs won the NFL Rookie of the Year in 1962 and 1965?

7. Who is the original four-year Bear from their first season in 1920 in his native Decatur, Illinois, better known for his long baseball career? (Hint: He managed the Brooklyn Dodgers to back-to-back pennants in 1952 and 1953.)

8. What is former Bear DE Trace Armstrong's real first name?
a. Armando
b. Henry
c. Neil
d. Raymond
e. Terrence

9. Name the 6'8" Hall of Fame defensive end from the University of Tennessee who spent 12 of his 17 seasons with the Bears.

10. True or False: Johnny Lujack, 1947 Heisman-winning QB and future College Football Hall of Fame inductee, played his entire NFL career with the Bears.

11. Which Bear holds the team record for yards rushing in a career, season, and game as well as the most career touchdowns?

   a. Jon Arnett
   b. Red Grange
   c. Bronko Nagurski
   d. Walter Payton
   e. Gale Sayers

12. Who was George Halas's co-coach and co-owner from 1922 to 1928?

   a. Red Grange
   b. Bill Harley
   c. C.C. Pyle
   d. Dutch Sternaman
   e. Joey Sternaman

13. What is coach Lovie Smith's full name?

14. Which Bear led the NFL in punt returns in 2010 and 2011 and is the NFL career leader in punt return average?

15. What 1946 Outland Trophy winner and Pro Football Hall of Fame member was a career Bear (1948–55), playing three different positions over that time (OT, DT, LB)?

   a. Dick Barwegan
   b. George Connor
   c. Chuck Drulis
   d. Bulldog Turner

16. Which member of the Bears' Super Bowl XX championship team competed in the 1988 Winter Olympics in Calgary?

   a. Mike Ditka
   b. Dave Duerson
   c. Willie Gault
   d. Jim McMahon
   e. Refrigerator Perry

17. Current coach in 2013 Marc Trestman was hired away from the CFL Montreal Alouettes, where he won two straight Grey Cup championships in 2009 and 2010. Did Trestman have any previous coaching experience in the NFL?

18. Name the 1938–43 Bear from Colgate and inductee into both the Pro and College Halls of Fame who retired from the NFL to pursue his medical practice.

    a. Danny Fortmann
    b. Sid Luckman
    c. George Musso
    d. Bronko Nagurski
    e. Bill Osmanski

19. Who was the left-handed QB who led the club in rushing with 968 yards in 1972, an NFL record for QBs at the time?

20. Match these Bear Hall of Fame stars with their alma mater:

    1. Dick Butkus   a. Arkansas
    2. Mike Ditka   b. Baylor
    3. Dan Hampton   c. Columbia
    4. Stan Jones   d. Illinois
    5. Sid Luckman   e. Jackson State
    6. Bronko Nagurski   f. Kansas
    7. Walter Payton   g. Maryland
    8. Gale Sayers   h. Minnesota
    9. Mike Singletary   i. Pitt
    10. Joe Stydahar   j. West Virginia

21. True or False: Bill McColl, a Chicago end from 1952 to 1959 and College Hall of Fame member, had a son who played in the NFL.

22. What Hall of Fame tackle spent the first three NFL seasons (1920–22) with the Rock Island Independents, then made All-NFL the next four years as a Bear?

23. The Bears traded for the original (1936) Heisman Trophy winner, back Jay Berwanger, from the Eagles, the team that drafted him. How long did he play for Chicago?

    a. never
    b. 3 games
    c. 1 season
    d. 4 years
    e. 10 years

24. What 1940s Bear had a second career playing pro basketball in the NBL from 1939 to 1946?

    a. Connie Mack Berry
    b. Ray Bray
    c. Aldo Forte
    d. George Halas
    e. Joe Stydahar

25. What Bears Hall of Fame fullback returned to the team in 1943 as a tackle, six years after he had retired?

26. What former Bears player succeeded George Halas as coach when the latter finally retired in 1968?

27. True or False: John Mangum, cornerback from 1990 to 1998, is a second-generation pro player.

28. Name the native Chicagoan and 1990 Lombardi Trophy–winning defensive tackle from Notre Dame who played for the Bears for six seasons?

29. The Bears' 2013 first-round draft pick is guard Kyle Long from the Oregon Ducks. Who is his NFL father?

    a. Chuck Long, QB
    b. Howie Long, DE
    c. Kevin Long, RB
    d. Terry Long, G

30. Who was the safety on the Bears' Super Bowl XX championship team who came to the team as an Ivy League grad from Yale?

CHICAGO BEARS ANSWERS

1. Mike Ditka.
2. a.
3. Gale Sayers won that award in 1966, 1967, and 1969.
4. True. Suhey was with Chicago from 1980 to 1989. His dad, Steve Suhey, spent two years with Pittsburgh, and his grandfather Bob Higgins (Steve's father-in-law) spent the first two years of the league (1920–21) with the Canton Bulldogs.
5. c.
6. Ronnie Bull (1962) and Gale Sayers (1975).
7. Chuck Dressen, a Decatur Staley/Chicago Bear from 1920 to 1923.
8. d.
9. Doug Atkins.
10. True, but he only lasted four years, retiring because of injuries.
11. d.
12. d. Sternaman was also a back on the team, as was his brother Joey. He sold his 50 percent of the team to Halas before the 1933 season.
13. Lovie Lee Smith. (Yes, that's his real first name.)
14. Devin Hester.
15. b.

16. c. Starting wide receiver Gault competed for the US bobsled team there. He also qualified for the 1980 US Olympic track squad, but the US boycotted those Moscow games to protest the USSR's invasion and occupation of Afghanistan at the time.

17. Yes. He was an assistant coach with eight different NFL teams (although the Bears were not one of them).

18. a.

19. Bobby Douglass.

20. 1. d; 2. i; 3. a; 4. g; 5. c; 6. h; 7. e; 8. f; 9. b; 10. j.

21. True. Son Milt McColl, now a doctor like his father, played linebacker for San Francisco (1981–87) and the LA Raiders (1988). Son Duncan McColl played for Stanford, as did his father and brother, and was Washington's fourth-round draft choice in 1977 but never played in the league.

22. Ed Healey.

23. a. Berwanger never signed a pro contract, deciding against a career in football.

24. a. (Note: Halas owned a Chicago team in that same basketball league.)

25. Bronko Nagurski.

26. Jim Dooley. He was the Bears' first-round draft choice in 1952, playing with the team until 1961. He coached the club from 1968 to 1971.

27. True. His father, John Mangum Sr., was an AFL Boston Patriot defensive tackle in 1967 and 1968. In addition, his brother Kris Mangum played tight end for Carolina in 1997 and 1998.

28. Chris Zorich.

29. b. His dad is broadcaster and Raiders defensive great Howie Long.

30. Gary Fencik.

CINCINNATI BENGALS

1. Who was the founder and first coach of the Bengals? (Hint: He was already in the Pro Football Hall of Fame when the team began play in 1968.)

2. Where did Marvin Lewis coach prior to taking the Bengals head coaching job in 2003?

3. What Bengals QB hails from little Augustana College (IL) and kept Super Bowl XVI close before losing to San Francisco?

4. Name the Bengal's 1976 first-round draft pick from Ohio State who had won back-to-back Heisman Trophies.

5. What ten-year Bengal receiver changed his last name to a variation of his uniform number, only to change it back in recent years (after moving to another team)?

6. What QB and tight end were Cincinnati teammates for two years, in the AFL and NFL, and each later became the Bengals head coach?

7. Who is the left-handed QB from the University of Maryland whose first name is actually Norman, played under a nickname, and both started and ended his NFL career in Cincinnati?

8. Who is the Bengals Hall of Fame tackle from USC who made All-Pro 11 straight seasons?

9. What Hall of Fame tackle was the 1981 AFC Coach of the Year for Cincinnati?

10. Who was Cincinnati's 2013 first-round draft choice?

11. What 1969 Outland Trophy winner (Penn State) and Bengal defensive tackle (from 1970 to 1974) is in both the College Hall of Fame and the Nashville Songwriters Hall of Fame and has a 1984 country-and-western songwriting Grammy award?

    a. Bill Bergey
    b. Royce Berry
    c. Ron Carpenter
    d. Mike Reid

12. Name the two-time Outland Trophy winner who was Cincy's first draft pick in 1983 and played center from 1983 to 1988?

13. Which Cincinnati QB holds the team record with 32 TD passes in a season?

    a. Ken Anderson
    b. Virgil Carter
    c. Andy Dalton
    d. Boomer Esiason
    e. Carson Palmer

14. When was the last time that a Bengal led the league in rushing yardage?

15. Which Bengal holds the franchise record with 132 points scored?

    a. Jim Breech
    b. Corey Dillon
    c. Shayne Graham
    d. Chad Ochocinco Johnson
    e. Mike Nugent

16. Who is the Bengals' all-time career rushing leader?

    a. James Brooks
    b. Corey Dillon
    c. Rudi Johnson
    d. Larry Kinnebrew
    e. Icky Woods

17. Who is the Bengals' one-season rushing leader?

    a. James Brooks
    b. Corey Dillon
    c. Rudi Johnson
    d. Larry Kinnebrew
    e. Icky Woods

18. Which former Bengal was the first to be inducted into the Hall of Fame in Canton, Ohio?

19. Which Bengal has the team single-season mark with 17 TDs scored?

    a. Corey Dillon
    b. Charlie Joiner
    c. Chad Ochocinco Johnson
    d. Carl Pickens
    e. Icky Woods

20. Which Cincinnati safety played in the Pro Bowl in three consecutive years (1988–90)?

    a. Lewis Billups
    b. Barney Bussey
    c. Rickey Dixon
    d. David Fulcher
    e. Solomon Wilcots

21. Match these Bengals with their alma mater:

    1. Cedric Benson   **a.** Arizona
    2. Lewis Billups   **b.** Auburn
    3. Jim Breech   **c.** California
    4. James Brooks   **d.** Georgia
    5. Andy Dalton   **e.** Idaho State
    6. David Fulcher   **f.** Nebraska
    7. A.J. Green   **g.** North Alabama
    8. Marvin Lewis   **h.** TCU
    9. Anthony Munoz   **i.** Texas
    10. Dave Rimington   **j.** USC

22. Who was the Bengals' first-round choice wide receiver in 1973 from San Diego State who spent his entire 12-year career with the team?

    a. Cris Collinsworth
    b. Isaac Curtis
    c. Charlie Joiner
    d. David Verser

23. What Cincinnati career interceptions leader led the AFC in that category in three different years?

   a. Tommy Casanova
   b. Leon Hall
   c. Bernard Jackson
   d. Lemar Parrish
   e. Ken Riley

24. Cincinnati had the NFL's overall first draft choice in both 1994 and 1995. Who did they choose?

25. What Notre Dame defensive lineman (and 1977 Outland and Maxwell awards winner) was the Cincinnati first-round draft pick in 1978, has three NFL brothers, and later found out he is the biological father of recent Steelers tackle Max Starks?

26. What 1976 Lombardi Award defensive tackle from the University of Houston played for the Bengals for six years (1977–82) and passed away from a heart condition at age 37 in 1992?

27. When was the first year the Bengals won their division and made the playoffs?

28. Which Bengals QB holds the NCAA division one single-game record with 716 passing yards?

   a. Andy Dalton
   b. Boomer Esiason
   c. David Klingler
   d. Carson Palmer

29. Which University of Oregon QB was the Bengals third overall draft selection in the first round of the 1999 NFL draft and is considered one of the all-time NFL draft busts?

30. Who was the Bengals defensive tackle who was the 1986 Outland Trophy winner from BYU and is now a co-owner of Utah of the Arena Football League?

CINCINNATI BENGALS ANSWERS

1. Paul Brown, former coach of the Cleveland Browns.
2. He had been the defensive coordinator of the Baltimore Ravens for several years, including during their Super Bowl XXXV win.
3. Kenny Anderson.
4. Running back Archie Griffin.
5. Chad "Ochocinco" Johnson.
6. Sam Wyche is the QB and Bruce Coslet the tight end.
7. Boomer Esiason.
8. Anthony Munoz.
9. Forrest Gregg.
10. Tyler Eifert, Notre Dame tight end.
11. d.
12. Dave Rimington.
13. e.
14. In 1968, rookie Paul Robinson led the AFL with 1,023.
15. e. In 2011.
16. b. Dillon had 8,061.
17. c. Johnson had 1,458 yards gained in 2005.
18. Charlie Joiner in 1996.
19. d. Pickens accomplished this in 1995.
20. d.
21. 1. i; 2. g; 3. c; 4. b; 5. h; 6. a; 7. d; 8. e; 9. j; 10. f.
22. b.
23. e. Riley had 65 career picks and led the AFC in 1976, 1982, and 1983.
24. RB Ki-Jana Carter in 1994 and DT Dan Wilkinson in 1995.
25. Ross Browner. His brother Jim was a teammate in Cincy for two years, and brothers Joey and Keith also were NFL contemporaries.
26. Wilson Whitley.

27. 1970, in their third year in existence (and first in the NFL after the merger). They were shutout by the Colts 17–0 in round one.

28. c. Klingler's unbelievable day occurred on December 2, 1990, for the University of Houston against Arizona State. He also picked up 16 more yards rushing during that game.

29. Akili Smith, who spent four years in Cincinnati and later played briefly for NFL Europe and the CFL.

30. Jason Buck.

CLEVELAND BROWNS

1. Which player did the Browns draft with the overall number one pick in 1999 who is considered one of the all-time draft blunders?

2. Who is the Browns Hall of Fame kicker, known as the Toe, who took a regular turn at tackle during the first half of his career and was the brother of an NBA player banned when his involvement in the point-fixing scandal at the University of Kentucky surfaced after several years?

3. What Pro and College Hall of Fame QB led the Browns to all four AAFC championships (1946–49), followed by the 1950 championship when the team merged into the NFL? (Hint: He later coached the US Coast Guard Academy and the Redskins.)

4. Who was drafted higher in the 1982 NFL draft, LB William "Chip" Banks or his USC college teammate, running back Marcus Allen?

5. True or False: Wide receiver and punt returner Eric Metcalf is a second-generation NFL player.

6. Who started the most games as Browns QB in 2012?

    a. Thaddeus Lewis
    b. Colt McCoy
    c. Seneca Wallace
    d. Brandon Weeden

7. Who holds the Browns' single-season receiving yards record?

    a. Josh Cribbs
    b. Braylon Edwards
    c. Ozzie Newsome
    d. Dennis Northcutt
    e. Webster Slaughter

8. Who was the Browns' first head coach after the franchise was revived in 1999?

    a. Bill Belichick
    b. Romeo Crennel
    c. Butch Davis
    d. Chris Palmer
    e. Marty Schottenheimer

9. True or False: The Browns were the only team in the 1946 fledgling AAFC that featured black players.

10. Which Hall of Fame running back was a sub for his first two years with the team (1964 and 1965)?

11. Which original Browns end, now in the Hall of Fame, played for coach Paul Brown as a freshman at Ohio State?

    a. Horace Gillom
    b. Dante Lavelli
    c. Mac Speedie
    d. John Yonaker

12. Name the Browns defensive tackle and end (1988–94) who was the 1989 AFC Defensive Player of the Year and went to six Pro Bowls. (Hint: He has a more famous NFL brother.)

13. Which back broke Jim Brown's single-game franchise rushing record with 286 yards on December 20, 2009?

14. Who was the QB for the "Kardiac Kids" Browns of the 1970s and 1980s who jumped to the New Jersey Generals of the USFL in 1984?

   a. Gary Danielson
   b. Bernie Kosar
   c. Paul McDonald
   d. Mike Pagel
   e. Brian Sipe

15. True or False: The Browns' 2011–12 coach, Pat Shurmur, is the son of the late Fritz Shurmur, NFL assistant for 24 years.

16. Who is the star defensive tackle who anchored Cleveland's defensive line in 1952 and from 1954 to 1964 and was an Outland Trophy winner from the University of Kentucky later inducted into the College Football Hall of Fame?

   a. Len Ford
   b. Bob Gain
   c. Bill Glass
   d. Jim Ray Smith
   e. Paul Wiggin

17. True or False: Head coach Rob Chudzinski was previously an assistant with the team.

18. For the second year in a row, the Browns had the number one overall NFL draft pick in 2000. Who did they select?

    a. Courtney Brown, DE

    b. JaJuan Dawson, WR

    c. Dennis Northcutt, WR

    d. Travis Prentice, RB

    e. Lewis Sanders, DB

19. Which rookie led Cleveland in rushing in 2012?

20. True or False: Cleveland holds a winning record against the Baltimore Ravens (the former Cleveland Browns).

21. True or False: Josh Cribbs, receiver and kick returner, is the son of former NFL and USFL star RB Joe Cribbs.

22. Who has the franchise's career, season, and game field goal records?

    a. Don Cockcroft

    b. Phil Dawson

    c. Lou Groza

    d. Matt Stover

23. Who played linebacker for the AAFC Browns in 1947–48 and is a College Hall of Fame coach, mainly from his days at Notre Dame (1964–74)?

24. Who was the last coach to lead Cleveland into the playoffs?

    a. Romeo Crennel

    b. Butch Davis

    c. Eric Mangini

    d. Chris Palmer

    e. Pat Shurmur

25. Who did Cleveland take as its first choice in the allocation draft (of veteran players) to restock the team in 1999?

   a. Raymond Jackson, S
   b. Jim Pyne, C
   c. Tarek Saleh, LB
   d. Mike Thompson, DT

26. True or False: Jim Shofner, Browns defensive back (1958–63) and interim coach (1990), is the brother of receiver Del Shofner.

27. Which Hall of Fame center won seven league championships as a Brown before beating Cleveland in the 1957 NFL championship game as a member of the Detroit Lions?

   a. Tom Catlin
   b. Frank Gatski
   c. Art Hunter
   d. John Morrow

28. Name the Browns QB, known for his brains, who, after the NFL, earned a PhD from his alma mater, Rice University, was Yale's athletic director, and taught math at Yale as well as Rice. (Hint: He ranks second all-time on the Cleveland TD passing list.)

29. Who was the 1979 Heisman-winning running back from USC whose mediocre five-year Browns career was later attributed to his admitting to cocaine use during his playing days?

30. Who was the Browns' first-round draft pick in 2013?

CLEVELAND BROWNS ANSWERS

1. Tim Couch, QB from Kentucky.
2. Lou Groza, the brother of Alex Groza.
3. Otto Graham.

4. Banks, whom Cleveland drafted with the third overall choice in the first round. Allen went tenth in that opening round. Chip Banks was voted the NFL Defensive Rookie of the Year after the season.

5. True. His father, Terry Metcalf, was an all-star back for the St. Louis Cardinals from 1973 to 1977, also playing for Washington and in the CFL.

6. d.

7. b. Edwards had 1,286 yards in 2007.

8. d.

9. True. Fullback Marion Motley and guard Bill Willis were the only two. The NFL LA Rams also had two black players, the first in the league in 14 years.

10. LeRoy Kelley, an eighth-round draft pick in 1964, mainly was a kickoff and punt returner until Jim Brown retired after 1965.

11. b.

12. Michael Dean Perry (brother of Refrigerator Perry).

13. Jerome Harrison.

14. e.

15. False. Fritz was Pat's uncle.

16. b.

17. True. Chudzinski was an assistant with the Browns in 2004 and again in 2007–08.

18. a.

19. Trent Richardson, number one draft choice.

20. False. The Ravens led the all-time series 20–7.

21. False.

22. b.

23. Ara Parseghian.

24. b. Davis guided the squad to a 9–7 record and a wild card berth in 2002. They lost to the Steelers in round one.

25. b. Pyne was tabbed from the Detroit Lions.

26. False. They're not related.

27. b.

28. Frank Ryan.

29. Charles White.

30. Barkevious "Keke" Mingo, defensive lineman from LSU, with the sixth overall pick.

DALLAS COWBOYS

1. Who was the coach Jerry Jones hired to take over the Cowboys after he bought the team in 1989?

   a. Dave Campo
   b. Mike Ditka
   c. Jimmy Johnson
   d. Barry Switzer
   e. Dave Wannstedt

2. What former Cowboy lineman was voted into the Hall of Fame in 2013?

3. What former Cowboy was the winner of *Dancing with the Stars* in 2006?

4. What player did the Cowboys select with the number one overall draft choice in 1989?

5. By what name was player Edward L. Jones most popularly known?

6. Who is the only Dallas head coach who played for the team?

7. True or False: The Cowboys are the most recent team to win back-to-back Super Bowls.

8. What is controversial LB Hollywood Henderson's real first name?

9. Who is the Dallas star running back from Yale whose son is an all-time NBA basketball great?

10. Who is the Dallas running back who holds the all-time NFL rushing record?

11. What longtime Cowboy receiver won two gold medals in track for the US Olympic team in 1964 in Tokyo?

12. Which former Cowboy defensive end is the franchise's career leader in sacks?

13. Who was the 1990 Outland Trophy–winning defensive tackle from the University of Miami whom Dallas selected with the number one overall draft choice in 1991?

14. How did Dallas acquire QB Tony Romo?
    a. NFL draft
    b. trade
    c. undrafted free agent
    d. waivers

15. Who was the highly touted University of Michigan All-American QB who started a game in 2004 and had a brief MLB career as a third baseman with the NY Yankees in 2002–03?

16. Which one of these Cowboys figures has not been inducted into the Hall of Fame in Canton, Ohio?

    a. Michael Irvin
    b. Jimmy Johnson
    c. Tom Landry
    d. Bob Lilly
    e. Roger Staubach

17. What defensive great from the University of Maryland won the Outland and Lombardi trophies in 1974, spent his entire career with the Cowboys, and is enshrined in both the Pro and College Football Halls of Fame?

18. Which former NFL number one overall draft pick did Tony Romo replace as starting QB in mid-2005?

19. Name the Cowboys' first starting QB in their first game on September 24, 1960.

    a. Don Heinrich
    b. Buddy Humphrey
    c. Eddie LeBaron
    d. Dandy Don Meredith

20. How many players changed hands in the epic midseason trade that sent running back Herschel Walker to the Vikings in October 1989?

21. In Super Bowl XII, Roger Staubach opposed and beat the QB he had supplanted as the Dallas starter several years before. Who was the former Cowboy playing as Denver's signal caller in that game?

22. Which one of these kickers for "America's Team" was born in the United States?

a. Chris Boniol
b. Toni Fritsch
c. Efren Herrera
d. Rafael Septien
e. Luis Zendejas

23. Who was the first Cowboy to gain more than 200 yards rushing in a game?

a. Tony Dorsett
b. Calvin Hill
c. Don Perkins
d. Emmitt Smith
e. Duane Thomas

24. Name the Cowboy who is the only Super Bowl MVP from a losing team.

25. How did Dallas obtain Hall of Fame QB Roger Staubach?

26. Where was LB Dat Nguyen born?

a. Arkansas
b. Cambodia
c. Laos
d. Texas
e. Vietnam

27. True of False: The NFL never had a team in Dallas prior to the birth of the Cowboys in 1960.

28. Who was the 1987 Outland Trophy–winning defensive tackle from Air Force who didn't reach the NFL until 1992 because of military commitment but nevertheless played for the Cowboys for nine years, including three Super Bowl wins?

29. Who was the Pro Bowl tight end on the Cowboys' three 1990s Super Bowl champs who was an All-American at the University of Wyoming?

   a. Eric Bjornson
   b. David LaFleur
   c. Jay Novacek
   d. Jay Saldi

30. How did Dallas acquire future Hall of Fame defensive lineman Randy White?

DALLAS COWBOYS ANSWERS

1. c. Jones hired his former University of Arkansas Razorbacks teammate Jimmy Johnson to replace Tom Landry, the franchise's original coach, who had been a Dallas institution for almost 30 years. Johnson had previously coached Oklahoma State and had taken the University of Miami to a national title.
2. Larry Allen. Allen was a Dallas guard from 1994 to 2005 and a frequent All-Pro selection.
3. Emmitt Smith. The Hall of Fame runner triumphed during the popular TV show's third season.
4. Troy Aikman, QB from UCLA. He orchestrated three Dallas Super Bowl wins and is now in the Hall of Fame.
5. Too Tall. Jones played his entire 15-season career (1974–78, 1980–89) with Dallas as a defensive end.
6. Jason Garrett, the current coach, was a backup QB for the Cowboys from 1992 to 1999.
7. False. Both Denver and New England have done it since Dallas won in Super Bowls XXVII and XXVIII.
8. Thomas.
9. Calvin Hill. His son is longtime Pistons star guard Grant Hill, now with the LA Clippers in 2013–14.
10. Emmitt Smith has 18,355 yards. He surpassed Walter Payton while still a Cowboy and has the team record with

17,162 yards gained, before leaving for his final two years in Arizona.

11. Bob Hayes, who is the only man to have won Olympic gold medals and a Super Bowl ring from Super Bowl VI (1971 season).

12. DeMarcus Ware with 117 sacks.

13. Russell Maryland.

14. c. Romo made the team as third-string QB and the holder in 2003 after not being drafted out of little Eastern Illinois.

15. Drew Henson.

16. b. Johnson was inducted into the College Hall of Fame as a coach in 2012, however.

17. Randy White, who was with Dallas from 1975 to 1988 and was a member of the Super Bowl XII champions.

18. Drew Bledsoe.

19. c. LeBaron was the former Washington QB acquired in a trade.

20. 18. Walker and four future draft picks were sent to Minnesota in exchange for five veterans and eight future draft picks.

21. Craig Morton.

22. a. Boniol comes from Alexandria, Louisiana. Fritsch was born in Austria and Herrera, Septien, and Zendejas are all from "South of the Border" (Mexico).

23. a. Hall of Famer Dorsett accomplished this feat in a 1977 game against the Eagles with a 206-yard day.

24. LB Chuck Howley, named MVP after the Cowboys' last-minute loss to the Colts in Super Bowl V.

25. He was a tenth-round future selection in the 1964 NFL draft. A graduate of Navy, he couldn't join Dallas until 1969 after he had completed his military commitment, which included a tour of duty in Vietnam during that war.

26. a. Nguyen, pronounced like *win*, was a Cowboy player (1999–2005) and assistant coach (2007–09). He was born in Arkansas but grew up in Texas. His parents are Vietnamese immigrants, and he is the first player with Vietnamese heritage to play in the league.

27. False. The Dallas Texans played in the league in 1952. Their home attendance was so weak that the owners forfeited the team to the NFL, which cancelled the remaining home games in midseason and had the team play on the road for the rest of the schedule. The Texans went 1–11 and faded into oblivion after the season.

28. Chad Hennings.

29. c.

30. In a 1975 midseason trade, the Cowboys sent their backup QB Craig Morton to the Giants, a team desperate for a signal caller, for a future draft pick that was turned into the number two overall selection in 1976. Dallas wisely picked White.

DENVER BRONCOS

1. What kicker played 15 of his 17 NFL seasons with Denver and is tied with Steve Christie for the NFL record for most career field goals in overtime (nine)? (Hint: He is Denver's all-time scoring leader.)

2. What pro team did John Elway play for prior to joining the Broncos?

3. How many times did Denver make the playoffs during its years in the AFL (1960–69)?

   a. 0
   b. 1
   c. 5
   d. 7
   e. 8

4. When was the first time Denver made the playoffs after joining the NFL in 1970?

   a. 1970
   b. 1972
   c. 1975
   d. 1977
   e. 1981

5. How did Denver obtain QB Peyton Manning?

6. What is CB Champ Bailey's real first name?

7. Who was the 2011 NFL Defensive Rookie of the Year (for both the AP and *Sports Illustrated*)?

8. True or False: Hall of Fame Bronco TE Shannon Sharpe and former NFL WR Sterling Sharpe are twins.

9. Name the three different backs that surpassed 1,000 yards rushing for the Broncos in 1998, 1999, and 2000.

10. Who is the Bronco running back from Syracuse University who led the AFC in rushing in both 1971 and 1972?

11. What receiver led the AFL in receptions in four of the league's first five years?

12. By what name was Denver's 1970s to early 1980s defensive unit known?

13. Who is original Bronco Al Carmichael's father?

14. Name the defensive back who led the AFL with 11 interceptions during its 1960 kickoff season?
    a. Goose Gonsoulin
    b. Jim McMillin
    c. Bob McNamara
    d. John Pyatt
    e. Bob Zeman

15. Did the Broncos' original coach, Frank Filchock (1960–61), ever play in the NFL?

16. What is John Elway's current job with the team?

17. Which QB became the main starter in 1999 after Elway retired?

    a. Bubby Brister
    b. Gus Frerotte
    c. Brian Griese
    d. Caleb Hanie
    e. Chris Miller

18. Name the Broncos' leader in career touchdowns:

    a. Terrell Davis
    b. Haven Moses
    c. Rod Smith
    d. Lionel Taylor
    e. Rick Upchurch

19. Which of these Broncos was not a number one draft pick by the club?

    a. Steve Atwater, DB
    b. Randy Gradishar, LB
    c. Tom Jackson, LB
    d. Rulon Jones, DE
    e. Marv Montgomery, T

20. Match these Broncos with their alma mater:

    1. Lyle Alzado   **a.** Florida
    2. John Elway   **b.** Georgia
    3. John Fox   **c.** Georgia Tech
    4. Tom Jackson   **d.** Louisville
    5. Knowshon Moreno   **e.** Missouri Southern
    6. Rod Smith   **f.** San Diego State
    7. Tim Tebow   **g.** Stanford
    8. Demaryius Thomas   **h.** Yankton

21. Which Denver defensive star led the NFL with 17 sacks in 2009, the team's single-season record?

22. For which other sport was original owner Bob Howsam known?

23. In what country was former DE Harald Hasselbach born?

    a. Austria
    b. Belgium
    c. Czech Republic
    d. Denmark
    e. Netherlands

24. True or False: Safety Steve Foley played his entire pro career with Denver.

25. True or False: Denver has a winning record (all-time) versus its three division rivals (all original AFL West clubs).

26. Which coach was fired despite a 9–5 record in 1976?

    a. Red Miller
    b. John Ralston
    c. Dan Reeves
    d. Jerry Smith

27. Who was the Broncos' first pick in the 2013 NFL draft?

28. Which QB did Elway replace as a rookie starter with Denver in 1983?

    a. Steve DeBerg
    b. Mark Hermann
    c. Gary Kubiak
    d. Craig Morton

29. True or False: Britton Colquitt is the fourth family member to be an NFL punter.

30. Did the Broncos win their first-ever regular season game (on September 9, 1960)?

DENVER BRONCOS ANSWERS

1. Jason Elam, a Bronco from 1993 to 2007.
2. Elway was a minor league baseball player for the Oneonta Yankees of the New York–Penn League in 1982. He batted .318 that season as an outfielder.
3. a. The Broncos were the only one of the original eight AFL clubs to never make the playoffs during that league's existence.
4. d. The Broncos finally got to the playoffs in 1977, after finishing their 18th season. They had the conference's best record and reached Super Bowl XII, where their charmed season came to an end, losing to the Dallas Cowboys. Denver made the playoffs again in both 1978 and 1979.
5. He was signed as a free agent in 2012 after missing the 2011 season with injuries.
6. Roland. Champ is actually his given middle name.
7. Von Miller.
8. False. They are brothers but Sterling is three years Shannon's senior in age.
9. Terrell Davis led the NFL with 2,008 yards in 1998, rookie Olandis Gary had 1,159 yards in 1999, and rookie Mike Anderson had 1,487 in 2000.
10. Floyd Little, a 2010 Hall of Fame inductee.
11. Lionel Taylor led the new league in catches from 1960 to 1963 and again in 1965. In 1961 he became the first player to surpass the 100-catch barrier.
12. Orange Crush Defense, named after the popular soda brand.
13. Songwriter Hoagy Carmichael ("Stardust" and many other songs) is the father of the 1960–61 halfback who had previously played in the NFL with Green Bay.

14. a. Gonsoulin was a Bronco for the team's first seven seasons, 1960–66.
15. Yes. He was a QB for Pittsburgh, Washington, the Giants, and the original Baltimore Colts from 1938 to 1950, missing some of those years while playing in Canada.
16. He is the executive vice president in charge of football operations.
17. c.
18. c. Smith tops the list with 71 TDs.
19. c. Jackson was drafted in the fourth round in 1973. He played all 14 of his NFL seasons with Denver and is now a well-known broadcaster with ESPN.
20. 1. h; 2. g; 3. f; 4. d; 5. b; 6. e; 7. a; 8. c.
21. Elvis Dumervil.
22. Baseball. He was GM of the St. Louis Cardinals (MLB, not NFL) from 1965 to 1966 and of the Cincinnati Reds from 1967 to 1977.
23. e. He was born in the city of Amsterdam.
24. False. Although Denver drafted him in 1975, he played one year with Jacksonville in the rival USFL before spending his entire NFL career (1976–86) with the Broncos. He had been a QB at Tulane.
25. False. They only have a winning record head-to-head with San Diego. Kansas City and Oakland have the advantage against them over the years.
26. b. Ralston later resurfaced in the USFL as the Oakland coach in 1983 and part of 1984.
27. Sylvester Williams, defensive tackle from North Carolina.
28. a. Elway started ten games, DeBerg five, and Kubiak one.
29. True. His father Craig, cousin Jimmy, and brother Dustin have all been punters in the league.
30. Yes. They beat the host Boston Patriots 13–10 in the franchise's first game that counted.

DETROIT LIONS

1. Which Lion set the new NFL record for catches in a season (since surpassed) in 1995?

2. How many relatives of Mel Farr, running back from 1967 to 1973, played in the NFL?

   a. 0
   b. 1
   c. 3
   d. 5
   e. 7

3. True or False: Former St. Louis Cardinals offensive star Mel Gray later played for the Lions.

4. What nickname did ABC *Monday Night Football* announcer Howard Cosell give to Lion punter Herman Weaver that stuck with him for the rest of his career?

5. Which Detroit coach was the 1991 NFL Coach of the Year?

   a. Monte Clark
   b. Wayne Fontes
   c. Darryl Rogers
   d. Bobby Ross

6. Name the Lions defensive tackle from 1958 to 1970 (except for 1963 when he was banned by the NFL for gambling) who was on ABC *Monday Night Football* as well as the TV comedy *Webster*, and whose brother played line for the Steelers, Bears, Lions, and Rams.

7. What Heisman Trophy winner followed that up by being NFL Rookie of the Year for the 1950 Lions? (Hint: College football has given the award for best running back named in his honor annually since 1990.)

8. Name the 13-year Detroit Hall of Fame middle linebacker who later was the team's coach for six years.

9. Which writer had a best seller with *Paper Lion*, about his real experiences trying to make the club as a QB during the 1963 training camp without any prior football background?

   a. Zane Grey
   b. Ring Lardner
   c. George Plimpton
   d. Damon Runyon

10. Name the 1955 Heisman-winning back and longtime Lion who was known by his nickname, a play on a popular cowboy movie and TV series?

11. Who is the career Lion defensive back and kick returner who made All-Pro seven straight times en route to the Pro and College Halls of Fame? (Hint: He later coached the 49ers.)

    a. Frankie Albert
    b. Jack Christiansen
    c. Monte Clark
    d. Dick LeBeau
    e. Steve Mariucci

12. What Lions coach from 1943 to 1947 had been the QB at Notre Dame during Knute Rockne's college playing career?

    a. Dutch Clark
    b. Gus Dorais
    c. Harry Gilmer
    d. George Wilson

13. Which Detroit receiver led the NFL with 1,681 reception yards in 2011?

    a. Nate Burleson
    b. Rashied Davis
    c. Calvin Johnson
    d. Titus Young

14. Who is the University of Nebraska defensive tackle Detroit picked first in the 2010 NFL draft?

15. What career Lion safety earned three NFL punting titles and nine Pro Bowl appearances on his way to the Hall of Fame?

    a. Jim David
    b. Don Doll
    c. Yale Lary
    d. Gary Lowe
    e. Bruce Maher

16. True or False: Bobby Layne was at QB when the Lions won their last NFL championship game in 1957.

17. Which Detroit QB had back-to-back seasons of more than 4,000 yards passing?

    a. Charlie Batch
    b. Jon Kitna
    c. Bill Munson
    d. Scott Mitchell
    e. Matthew Stafford

18. Which Detroit running back was the first to surpass the 1,000-yard barrier in franchise history?

  a. Amos Marsh
  b. Steve Owens
  c. Barry Sanders
  d. Billy Sims
  e. Altie Taylor

19. Which QB holds the team record with 5,038 passing yards and 41 TDs in a season?

  a. Charlie Batch
  b. Jon Kitna
  c. Bobby Layne
  d. Scott Mitchell
  e. Matthew Stafford

20. What Lion holds the NFL record with 14 consecutive games of more than 100 rushing yards?

  a. Jahvid Best
  b. Dutch Clark
  c. John Henry Johnson
  d. Barry Sanders
  e. Billy Sims

21. Thanksgiving and football in Detroit have been an NFL tradition since 1934. Do the Lions have a winning or losing record on "Turkey Day"?

22. Who was the 6'5" Heisman winner from Notre Dame who played defensive end, tight end, and fullback in his Lions career (1950–57) and is in the College Football Hall of Fame?

a. Charlie Ane
b. Cloyce Box
c. Lou Creekmur
d. Leon Hart
e. Jim Martin

23. Which Lion tackle (1937–38), known as Horse in his playing days, is in the College Hall of Fame and was the first president (and minority owner) of baseball's LA Angels in 1961, as well as being a minority owner and exec with the LA Rams during that same period?

a. Ox Emerson
b. Jack Johnson
c. Bob Reynolds
d. Alex Wojciechowicz

24. The Lions had the NFL Rookie of the Year in consecutive years, 1959 (a fullback) and 1960 (an end). Name them.

25. Did 1948–50 Lions coach (and 1934–47 Indiana University coach) Bo McMillin ever play in the NFL?

26. What Lions coach in 1939 took the club to a 6–5 record in his only year with the team? (Hint: He had coached the 1937 LA Bulldogs of the rival AFL to an undefeated season after the NFL turned that team down for being too far away from other league teams. He was better known for his college coaching career at USC and Tulsa.)

27. Who is the owner of the Lions, and who was his very famous inventor-industrialist grandfather?

28. Name the only Lions coach who was also the head coach at the University of Michigan.

29. Which QB was the 1989 Heisman winner from the University of Houston but was mainly a backup in his four years with Detroit (1990–93)?

    a. Bob Gagliano
    b. Erik Kramer
    c. Rodney Peete
    d. Andre Ware

30. Name the Lions first-round draft pick in 2013 who hadn't played football until his junior year of college?

DETROIT LIONS ANSWERS

1. Herman Moore. Moore had 123 receptions to break the record of 122 set by Minnesota's Cris Carter the previous season. Moore's mark is still the Detroit record.
2. d. Farr's cousin Lem Barney, cornerback, was his Lions teammate for his entire NFL career. His older brother Miller Farr played cornerback for Denver, San Diego, and Houston in the AFL, the St. Louis Cards in the AFL, and Florida in the rival WFL from 1965–74. Cousin Jerry LeVias played for the Oilers and Chargers. Mel's two sons, Mel Jr. (LA Rams, 1989) and Mike (Detroit and New England, 1990–93), followed in his footsteps. Another of Mel's cousins was the late Motown legend, singer-songwriter Marvin Gaye. In fact Mel Farr and Barney appeared as backup singers on Gaye's album *What's Goin On.*
3. False. While Detroit had a player of the same name from 1989–93, that was a different player. The St. Louis receiver, Mel D. Gray from the University of Missouri, retired in 1982. Detroit's kick returner and running back Mel J. Gray was from Purdue.
4. Thunderfoot.
5. b.
6. Alex Karras, brother of Ted Karras.
7. Doak Walker.
8. Joe Schmidt.

9. c. Novelist Grey incidentally played minor league baseball.
10. Howard "Hopalong" Cassady (1956–61 and 1963).
11. b.
12. b.
13. c.
14. Ndamukong Suh.
15. c.
16. False. Layne had broken his leg a few games before, and Tobin Rote was the signal caller that led them to victory.
17. b. Kitna accomplished this in 2006 and 2007.
18. b. Owens, the 1969 Heisman winner from the Oklahoma Sooners, had 1,035 yards in 1971.
19. e. Stafford set those records in 2011.
20. d. Sanders did this in 1997.
21. Losing. Their Thanksgiving record is 35–38, all in home games.
22. d.
23. c.
24. Nick Pietrosante, 1959, and Gail Cogdill, 1960.
25. Yes. McMillin was a QB for the Milwaukee Badgers and Cleveland Indians, two long-defunct clubs, in 1922 and 1923.
26. Gus Henderson.
27. William Clay Ford, whose grandfather Henry Ford founded Ford Motors. The family name has been synonymous with Detroit for a century. William Clay Ford died on March 9, 2014.
28. Gary Moeller, who was the interim coach for Detroit for the second half of 2000 after heading the Wolverines from 1990 to 1994.
29. d.
30. Ezekial "Ziggy" Ansah, a defensive lineman/linebacker from BYU, who was born in Ghana.

GREEN BAY PACKERS

1. Coach Vince Lombardi was a member of a famous offensive line as a college player at Fordham in the mid-1930s? What was that line's nickname?

2. What team did Green Bay narrowly beat at Lambeau Field on December 31, 1967, in the "Ice Bowl" to advance to Super Bowl II?

3. How did the Packers acquire receiver Donald Driver?
   a. first-round draft pick
   b. free agency
   c. seventh-round pick
   d. traded for him
   e. waivers

4. Name the Hall of Fame Packer who was the first in the NFL to reach over 1,000 receiving yards in a season (1942).

5. Who was the 1972 NFC Coach of the Year? (Hint: He was mainly known as a college coach.)

6. Which QB holds the team's one-game records for six TD passes and 480 yards.

    a. Brett Favre
    b. Matt Flynn
    c. Arnie Herber
    d. Aaron Rodgers
    e. Bart Starr

7. True or False: Green Bay has more NFL championships than any other franchise.

8. Match these Green Bay Hall of Fame players with their alma mater:

1. Johnny Blood	**a.** Alabama
2. Tony Canadeo	**b.** Bucknell
3. Arnie Herber	**c.** Gonzaga
4. Clark Hinkle	**d.** Regis
5. Don Hutson	**e.** St. John's (MN)
6. James Lofton	**f.** Stanford
7. Reggie White	**g.** Tennessee

9. Who is the Packers' career rushing leader?

    a. John Brockington
    b. Ahman Green
    c. Paul Hornung
    d. Dorsey Levens
    e. Jim Taylor

10. Which coach replaced Vince Lombardi in 1968 when the latter gave up the coach's job but remained the GM?

    a. Phil Bengtson
    b. Dan Devine
    c. Forrest Gregg
    d. Ray McLean
    e. Bart Starr

11. Where was kicker Chester Marcol born?

12. Which Packer wrote the best seller *Instant Replay*, the chronicle of a football season?

13. Which Green Bay coach has the most career franchise victories?

    a. Mike Holmgren
    b. Curly Lambeau
    c. Mike McCarthy
    d. Mike Sherman
    e. Bart Starr

14. Match these 1960s Packers dynasty Hall of Famers with their alma mater:

1. Herb Adderly	**a.** Alabama
2. Willie Davis	**b.** Grambling
3. Forrest Gregg	**c.** Illinois
4. Paul Hornung	**d.** LSU
5. Henry Jordan	**e.** Michigan State
6. Ray Nitschke	**f.** Notre Dame
7. Jim Ringo	**g.** SMU
8. Bart Starr	**h.** Syracuse
9. Jim Taylor	**i.** USC
10. Willie Wood	**j.** Virginia

15. Who is the Packers' career leader in sacks?

    a. Kabeer Gbaja-Biamila
    b. Tim Harris
    c. Vonnie Holiday
    d. Clay Matthews

16. How did Green Bay obtain Brett Favre?

a. draft choice
b. free agent
c. traded a draft pick
d. waivers

17. Who was the Packer starting QB, nicknamed Magic, for several years prior to Brett Favre?

18. True or False: The 1960s dynasty teammates Jerry Kramer (G) and Ron Kramer (TE) are brothers.

19. Which star running back from the 2012 national champion Alabama Crimson Tide did Green Bay pick in 2013's second round?

20. What back holds the single-season Packers rushing record?
    a. John Brockington
    b. Ahman Green
    c. MacArthur Lane
    d. Terdell Middleton
    e. Jim Taylor

21. Which Packer was voted MVP when the team won Super Bowl XLV?
    a. Donald Driver
    b. Jermichael Finley
    c. Clay Matthews
    d. Aaron Rodgers
    e. James Starks

22. Who replaced Curly Lambeau as Green Bay coach in 1950?

    a. Lisle Blackbourn
    b. Vince Lombardi
    c. Scooter McLean
    d. Gene Ronzani

23. When was the first time a Packer reached 1,000 yards rushing?

24. True or False: QB Anthony Dilweg, the Pack's third-round draft pick in 1989 out of Duke, was a "legacy" player, his relative having played for the team previously.

25. Green Bay was the first team to win three straight NFL championships. In what years did they accomplish this?

26. What coach did Vince Lombardi replace at Green Bay?

    a. Lisle Blackbourn
    b. Hugh Devore
    c. Scooter McLean
    d. Gene Ronzani

27. True or False: Coach Mike Holmgren was an NFL player.

28. What former Green Bay Pro Bowl safety was both an All-American and an Academic All-American for the University of Arizona in 1987?

29. Which tackle was the 1989 second overall choice in the first round and is considered one of the all-time draft busts?

30. What 1935–37 Packer fullback became the New York AFL GM and drafted his own son for that team in 1965?

a. Charley Brock
b. Cecil Isbell
c. George Sauer
d. Ed Smith

GREEN BAY PACKERS ANSWERS

1. The Seven Blocks of Granite. Lombardi was a guard, and fellow Pro Football Hall of Famer Alex Wojciechowicz was the center.
2. The Dallas Cowboys lost by a 21–17 score.
3. c. Driver was selected in the seventh round in 1999 and spent 14 years with Green Bay.
4. Don Hutson, who had 1,211 yards in an 11-game season.
5. Dan Devine.
6. b. Flynn, a backup playing because the Packers already clinched their playoff spot and were resting starters including Aaron Rodgers, had his career day on New Year's Day 2012 versus Detroit.
7. True. With 11 championships, Green Bay has a lead on the Bears, Giants, and Cowboys, who have all won eight times.
8. 1. e; 2. c; 3. d; 4. b; 5. a; 6. f; 7. g.
9. b. Green had 8,322 yards in eight seasons with the Pack.
10. a. Bengtson had been an assistant under Lombardi.
11. Poland. Marcol was the Packers' kicker from 1972 to 1980.
12. Jerry Kramer, guard, with help from sportswriter Dick Schaap, wrote the 1968 book, which gave the player's perspective of the 1967 championship season.
13. b. Lambeau, the man the stadium is named for, has 212 career wins in 29 years with the franchise. He ranks fourth on the all-time NFL list with 229 wins, coaching the Cards and Skins after leaving Green Bay.
14. 1. e; 2. b; 3. g; 4. f; 5. j; 6. c; 7. h; 8. a; 9. d; 10. i.
15. a. KGB had 74.5 sacks from 2000 to 2008.
16. c. The Packers traded their 1992 first-round selection to get Favre from Atlanta, where the 1991 rookie had four total passes while spending most of the year on the bench. The results were two interceptions and two incompletions.

17. Don Majkowski.
18. False. They weren't related.
19. Eddie Lacy.
20. b. Green had 1,883 yards in 2003.
21. d.
22. d. Ronzani spent his playing career with the Chicago Bears but went to college at nearby Marquette.
23. 1949, when Tony Canadeo had 1,052.
24. True. Dilweg was a Packer in 1989 and 1990, and his grandfather, Lavie Dilweg, was a Green Bay end from 1927 to 1934.
25. 1929, 1930, and 1931, before the NFL had divisions or playoff games.
26. c.
27. False. Holmgren was a backup QB in college. He never made the cut in the NFL, though he was an eighth-round draft pick of the St. Louis Cardinals in 1970. The Cards cut him in training camp, and so did the Jets soon after.
28. Chuck Cecil.
29. Tony Mandarich, projected for NFL stardom when the Pack selected him, was a holdout as a rookie, and his alleged drug, alcohol, and steroid use are cited as the reason for his less-than-mediocre three seasons in Green Bay. He made a three-year comeback with Indianapolis (1996–98) after four years out of the NFL, but injuries ended his playing days for good.
30. c. His son George Jr. led all receivers with 133 yards in Super Bowl III.

HOUSTON TEXANS

1. The Texans were given the number one overall choice in the 2002 NFL draft for their expansion season. Who did they choose?

2. Houston set a dubious NFL record for a season in the 2002 expansion year. What was it?

   a. fewest points scored
   b. fewest wins
   c. most fumbles lost
   d. most punts

3. When was the first year that the Texans earned a playoff berth?

   a. 2004
   b. 2007
   c. 2008
   d. 2011
   e. 2012

4. Who was the QB when Houston won its first-ever playoff game?

a. David Carr
b. Sage Rosenfels
c. Matt Schaub
d. T.J. Yates

5. The Texans had the NFL's oldest player in 2011. Who was he?

6. True or False: Coach Gary Kubiak played in the NFL.

7. Who are the only Texans to win (Associated Press) Rookie of the Year, offense or defense (pick two)?

a. David Carr
b. Brian Cushing
c. Andre Johnson
d. DeMeco Ryans
e. J.J. Watt

8. Who was the first Texan to lead the NFL in rushing?

9. How did Houston acquire star QB Matt Schaub?

a. first-round draft pick
b. free agency
c. seventh-round draft pick
d. trade
e. waivers

10. Match these Texans with their alma mater:

1. Connor Barwin	**a.** Abilene Christian
2. Arian Foster	**b.** Cincinnati
3. Bradie James	**c.** LSU
4. Andre Johnson	**d.** Miami
5. Gary Kubiak	**e.** North Carolina State
6. Danieal Manning	**f.** Tennessee
7. Matt Schaub	**g.** Texas A&M
8. J.J. Watt	**h.** Virginia
9. Mario Williams	**i.** Wisconsin

11. Who was the Texans' original coach?

12. What was Gary Kubiak's job prior to becoming Houston's head coach in 2006?

13. Who was the running back who gained 942 yards in 2011, second on the team to Arian Foster?

14. When did Matt Schaub lead the NFL in passing yards?

15. Who was Houston's first-round draft choice in 2013?

16. Name the Texans lineman who won AFC Defensive Player of the Year as well as the AP NFL Defensive Player of the Year in 2012.

17. What receiver holds every Texans receptions record (game, season, and career)?

18. Which Texan tied an NFL record by scoring two interception TDs in a game during the inaugural 2002 season?

19. Who holds the team record for interceptions in a game?

  a. Jason Allen
  b. Quintin Demps
  c. Aaron Glenn
  d. Danieal Manning
  e. Glover Quin

20. True or False: Arian Foster was a Houston first-round draft pick.

21. Whom did Houston select with its 2012 first-round draft choice?

  a. Brandon Brooks, G
  b. Ben Jones, C
  c. Keshawn Martin, WR
  d. Whitney Mercilus, LB
  e. DeVier Posey, WR

22. The Texans' first regular season game was at home against their cross-state rivals, the Dallas Cowboys, on September 8, 2002. Who won?

23. Whom did Houston select first in the 2002 expansion draft?

  a. Tony Boselli, Jaguars T
  b. Aaron Glenn, Jets CB
  c. Jermaine Lewis, Ravens WR
  d. Jamie Sharper, Ravens LB
  e. Danny Wuerfel, Bears QB

24. For how many years was the city of Houston without a major league football franchise between the Oilers' leaving for Tennessee and the Texans' first game?

25. Who was the Texans defensive back selected to start for the AFC in the 2013 Pro Bowl (2012 season)?

26. Who are the Texans' career and single-season sack leaders?

27. What safety did Houston sign away from the champion Ravens as a 2013 free agent?

28. What University of South Carolina safety was the Texans' second draft pick in 2013?

29. Which Texan holds the NFL record for most fumble recoveries in a season?

30. Which Texan led the team in scoring for eight consecutive seasons?
    a. Kris Brown
    b. Ron Dayne
    c. Andre Johnson
    d. Neil Rackers
    e. Domanick Williams

HOUSTON TEXANS ANSWERS

1. David Carr, QB from Fresno State, who became an immediate starter as a rookie.
2. d. The Texans set an all-time record with 116 punts, breaking the 1981 Bears record by two.
3. d. Houston won its division and advanced to the playoffs for the first time in its tenth season.
4. d. Yates became the QB late in 2011 when Schaub was injured and led the squad to a 31–10 trouncing of Cincinnati in the franchise's first-ever playoff contest.
5. Punter Matt Turk, who started that year with the Jaguars, was 43 years old in 2011.

6. True. Kubiak was a Denver QB from 1983 to 1991, backing up John Elway.

7. b and d. Ryans (LB) won the Defensive Rookie award in 2006. Cushing (another LB) won the same award in 2009.

8. Arian Foster topped the league with 1,616 yards in 2010.

9. d. Schaub came to the Texans from Atlanta in exchange for two second-round draft picks in March 2007. He had been Michael Vick's backup with the Falcons for several years.

10. 1. b; 2. f; 3. c; 4. d; 5. g; 6. a; 7. h; 8. i; 9. e.

11. Dom Capers, who had also been the first-ever coach of expansion Carolina.

12. Kubiak had been the Denver Broncos' offensive coordinator.

13. Ben Tate came within reach of the thousand-yard plateau but slipped to 279 yards in 2012.

14. Schaub led the league in 2009 when he had 4,770 yards through the air.

15. Wide receiver DeAndre Hopkins from Clemson.

16. J.J. Watt.

17. Andre Johnson. He is tied for most receptions in a game with Kevin Walter, 12. He led the NFL in receiving yards in 2008 and 2009, and in most catches in 2006 and 2008.

18. Aaron Glenn (DB) had two picks for TDs on December 8 that year. He tied a record held by 21 others at the time.

19. e. Quin picked off three Titans passes in a 2010 game.

20. False. Foster was an undrafted free agent in 2009 and a practice squad player before being activated in midseason.

21. d. Mercilus was tabbed first, from the University of Illinois.

22. Houston beat Dallas 19–10.

23. a. Boselli was Houston GM Charley Casserly's first expansion choice. He was injured in training camp and never played a down for the team before retiring.

24. Four years. The Oilers (now the Titans) left Houston after 1997. The Texans were awarded an NFL franchise in 1999 but didn't take the field until 2002.

25. Cornerback Johnathan Joseph.

26. Mario Williams had 53 sacks in his six years in Houston before he left as a free agent in 2012. J.J. Watt broke Williams's one-year club sacks record with 20.5 in 2012.

27. Ed Reed.
28. D.J. Swearinger.
29. David Carr. The QB had 12 recoveries in 2002, all on his own fumbles.
30. a. Kicker Kris Brown topped the team scoring list during all of its first eight seasons, 2002–09.

INDIANAPOLIS COLTS

1. Marvin Harrison holds the Colts' single-season and career receiving records. How did the Colts acquire him?
   - **a.** Arena League
   - **b.** eighth-round draft pick
   - **c.** first-round draft pick
   - **d.** trade
   - **e.** waivers

2. The Baltimore Colts had the first overall pick in the first combined NFL-AFL college draft in 1967. Who did they pick?

3. Who is the Hall of Fame coach who was the 1968 NFL Coach of the Year from Baltimore?

4. Who did Indianapolis pick the last time they had the number one overall NFL draft choice?

5. Who is the Hall of Fame end who played his entire 13-year NFL career with the Baltimore Colts and later coached New England in their first Super Bowl appearance?

6. Who is the Hall of Fame defensive tackle nicknamed Fatso who played for both the 1950 original (and defunct) Balti-

more Colts from the AAFC merger and the 1953 expansion Baltimore Colts?

7. Who is the Outland and Lombardi trophy–winning defensive tackle whom Indianapolis selected as the number one overall choice in 1992?

8. Who is the longtime Baltimore Colts QB whose father played halfback in the NFL from 1948 to 1955?

9. True or False: Hall of Fame DE Gino Marchetti played his entire career with the Baltimore Colts.

10. Did Baltimore kicker and defensive lineman Lou Michaels (1964–70) have a brother in the NFL?

11. Who is the College and Pro Hall of Fame guard/tackle who spent his whole NFL career (1957–67) as a Baltimore Colt?
    a. Buzz Nutter
    b. Jim Parker
    c. Sherman Plunkett
    d. George Preas
    e. Alex Sandusky

12. What QB picked in the ninth round of the 1955 draft by Pittsburgh, where he was cut, joined Baltimore the next year on his way to becoming one of the all-time greats?

13. Which of these Colts was first to be inducted into the Hall of Fame?
    a. Ray Berry
    b. Art Donovan
    c. Gino Marchetti
    d. Lenny Moore
    e. Johnny Unitas

14. Which Colt running back holds the franchise's career, season, and game rushing records?

   a. Joseph Addai
   b. Eric Dickerson
   c. Marshall Faulk
   d. Edgerrin James
   e. Lenny Moore

15. Who was the last Baltimore Colts coach, as well as being the first Indianapolis coach?

16. Who is the Colts franchise's all-time scoring leader?

17. Since moving to Indianapolis, which coach has the most career victories?

   a. Jim Caldwell
   b. Tony Dungy
   c. Lindy Infante
   d. Ron Meyer
   e. Jim Mora

18. Overall, which coach has the most franchise victories (Baltimore years included)?

   a. Dungy
   b. Weeb Ewbank
   c. Ted Marchibroda
   d. Mora
   e. Don Shula

19. Match these Hall of Fame Colts with their alma mater:

1. Eric Dickerson   a. Boston College
2. Art Donovan   b. Louisville
3. Weeb Ewbank   c. Miami of Ohio
4. Marshall Faulk   d. Ohio State
5. Gino Marchetti   e. Penn State
6. Lenny Moore   f. San Diego State
7. Jim Parker   g. San Francisco
8. Johnny Unitas   h. SMU

20. True or False: Dwight Freeney is the Colts' career sacks leader.

21. Which receiver holds the franchise's season record of 1,510 reception yards?

22. Which Colts QB appeared in the most games during 2011, when Peyton Manning was injured?

    a. Kerry Collins
    b. Dan Orlovsky
    c. Curtis Painter
    d. Drew Stanton

23. True or False: Peyton Manning led the NFL in TD passes during all his years with the Colts.

24. The Colts had the NFL Rookie of the Year in 1955 (FB), 1956 (HB), and 1958 (end). Who were these three players?

25. What Colts' number one draft pick in 1953 and future College Hall of Fame running back signed with Edmonton of the Canadian League and didn't get to play for the Colts until 1956 (for a single season)?

a. L.G. Dupre
b. Buck McPhail
c. Jim Sears
d. Billy Vessels
e. Dick Young

26. Who is the 1964 Maxwell Award–winning guard/tackle from Penn State who played his entire ten-year NFL career with the Colts in Baltimore?

27. Name the 1982 Colts first-round draft pick QB from Ohio State (fourth overall) whose promising NFL career was cut short by his compulsive gambling, including being suspended for the entire 1983 season for that activity.

28. Indy's first draft pick in 2013 is Bjoern Werner, Florida State defensive lineman. He came to the United States initially as a high school exchange student. Where is he from?

a. Austria
b. Denmark
c. Germany
d. Sweden

29. Which former Colts QB was a member of Arizona State's 1981 NCAA baseball champions?

30. Who was the last of the Baltimore Colts to retire from the NFL?

INDIANAPOLIS COLTS ANSWERS

1. c. Harrison was Indy's first-round choice in 1996, out of Syracuse University. He played for the team from 1996 to 2008.
2. Michigan State defensive lineman Bubba Smith.
3. Don Shula.
4. QB Andrew Luck in 2012.

5. Raymond Berry.
6. Art Donovan.
7. Steve Emtman.
8. Bert Jones, son of Dub Jones.
9. False. Marchetti came into the league in 1952 with the Dallas Texans, a team that folded after the season.
10. Yes. Walt Michaels, linebacker for Green Bay, Cleveland, and New York in the AFL, and future Jets and USFL New Jersey Generals coach, was his brother.
11. b.
12. Johnny Unitas.
13. b.
14. d.
15. Frank Kush.
16. Mike Vanderjagt with 995 points.
17. b, with 92.
18. a. Still Dungy. Shula, the NFL's all-time coaching wins leader, ranks second with 73 (while in Baltimore). Marchibroda also has a combined total of 73 in two stints, first in Baltimore and later in Indy.
19. 1. h; 2. a; 3. c; 4. f; 5. g; 6. e; 7. d; 8. b.
20. True. He has 107.5.
21. Reggie Wayne, in 2007.
22. c. Painter started eight times and appeared in nine games. (Collins started the season.)
23. False. Manning led the NFL twice—in 2004 and 2006. He did lead the AFC in TD passes six times in his Indianapolis years.
24. Alan Ameche (1955), Lenny Moore (1956), and Jimmy Orr (1958).
25. d.
26. Glenn Ressler.
27. Art Schlichter.
28. c. He was born and raised in Berlin.
29. Mike Pagel, who was a substitute outfielder.
30. Punter Rohn Stark, who retired after 1997, spent the first 13 of his 16 NFL seasons with Baltimore/Indianapolis.

JACKSONVILLE JAGUARS

1. Who holds the Jags' career and single-season receiving records for both catches and yardage?

2. Who has the team record for most passes caught in a game?
   a. Justin Blackmon
   b. Maurice Jones-Drew
   c. Keenan McCardell
   d. Jimmy Smith
   e. Mike Thomas

3. Who was the Jaguars' original coach in 1995?

4. Which QB holds the Jags' yardage records for a career, season, and game?
   a. Mark Brunnell
   b. Blaine Gabbert
   c. David Garrard
   d. Byron Leftwich

5. In what year did Jacksonville first win its division?

6. Who was the Jaguars' interim coach for the last five games in 2011 after Jack Del Rio was fired?

   a. Louis Clark
   b. Joe Cullen
   c. Mark Lamping
   d. Greg Olsen
   e. Mel Tucker

7. True or False: Safety Dawan Landry has a brother who also plays in the NFL.

8. What Jacksonville back led the NFL with 1,606 rushing yards in 2011?

9. Who was the Jags' second overall pick in the first round of the 2013 NFL draft?

10. Who is the franchise's single-season and lifetime sacks leader?

    a. Tony Brackens
    b. Kevin Hardy
    c. John Henderson
    d. Joel Smeenge
    e. Paul Spicer

11. Who has been the team's center since 2000?

12. Who is the Jags' career scoring leader?

    a. Mike Hollis
    b. Maurice Jones-Drew
    c. Josh Scobee
    d. Jimmy Smith
    e. Fred Taylor

13. Match these Jaguars with their alma mater:

1.	Tony Boselli	a.	Florida
2.	Mark Brunnell	b.	Jackson State
3.	Blaine Gabbert	c.	Louisiana Tech
4.	Maurice Jones-Drew	d.	Marshall
5.	Byron Leftwich	e.	Missouri
6.	Brad Meester	f.	Northern Iowa
7.	Josh Scobee	g.	Tennessee
8.	Jimmy Smith	h.	UCLA
9.	James Stewart	i.	USC
10.	Fred Taylor	j.	Washington

14. Who is the Jaguars' all-time leading rusher (career)?

a. Maurice Jones-Drew
b. Natrone Means
c. James Stewart
d. Fred Taylor

15. Who was the Jaguars' first-ever draft choice in the college draft (1995)?

a. Steve Beuerlein, QB
b. Tony Boselli, DT
c. Brian DeMarco, T
d. Bryan Schwartz, LB
e. James Stewart, RB

16. Original Jaguar LB Bernard Carter (1995) has a brother who had a much longer NFL career (1995–2008). Who is his brother?

a. Andre Carter, DE
b. Cris Carter, WR
c. Delone Carter, RB
d. Kevin Carter, DE
e. Quinton Carter, S

17. Prior to the Jaguars, did Jacksonville ever have a major pro football team?

18. True or False: Offensive coordinator Bob Bratkowski played in the NFL.

19. What is coach Gus Bradley's actual first name:
    a. August
    b. Casey
    c. Chad
    d. Gustav
    e. Paul

20. Who is the only Jaguar to win the Pro Bowl MVP award?
    a. Tony Boselli
    b. Mark Brunell
    c. Maurice Jones-Drew
    d. Jimmy Smith
    e. Marcus Stroud

21. Which Jaguar led the NFL in scoring in 1997 with 134 points?

22. Which defensive back holds the team record with eight interceptions in a season?
    a. Aaron Beasley
    b. Derek Cox
    c. Donovan Darius
    d. Rashean Mathis
    e. Marlon McCree

23. Did the Jags ever have a midseason trade?

24. True or False: Early Jaguar defensive lineman John Jurkovic was born in Croatia.

25. Who is the only Jaguar player to attend the University of Jacksonville?

26. Where was owner Shahid Khan born?

    a. Chicago
    b. India
    c. Jacksonville
    d. Pakistan
    e. Quebec

27. True or False: Coach Mike Mularkey never played in the NFL.

28. Who is 2012 defensive back Aaron Ross's wife?

    a. Allyson Felix
    b. Sanya Richards
    c. Diana Ross
    d. Tracee Ellis Ross

29. Did new GM David Caldwell ever play in the NFL?

30. Who has been the Jaguars' radio play-by-play announcer since the team started in 1995?

    a. Deron Cherry
    b. Jeff Lageman
    c. Matt Robinson
    d. Brian Sexton

JACKSONVILLE JAGUARS ANSWERS

1. Jimmy Smith. Smith played for the team from 1995 to 2005 with 116 catches (NFL leader) and 1,244 yards in 1999, and 862 receptions and 12,287 yards over his career.
2. c. McCardell caught 16 passes on October 20, 1996.

3. Tom Coughlin. Coughlin, who got Jacksonville into the playoffs four consecutive times starting with their second year of competition in 1996, has gone on to greater success by winning two Super Bowls as coach of the Giants. He was the 1996 NFL Coach of the Year.

4. a.

5. 1998, with an 11–5 record.

6. e.

7. True. His brother LaRon, also a safety, played for Washington and more recently has been with the Jets.

8. Maurice Jones-Drew.

9. Texas A&M Aggies tackle Luke Joeckel.

10. a.

11. Brad Meester, who retired after the 2013 season. He is the team record holder with 14 seasons and most career games.

12. c. 848 points.

13. 1. i; 2. j; 3. e; 4. h; 5. d; 6. f; 7. c; 8. b; 9. g; 10. a.

14. d. 11,271 yards in 11 seasons (1998–2008).

15. b (second overall choice). Beuerlein was the first pick of the expansion draft.

16. d. Kevin Carter played for St. Louis, Tennessee, Miami, and Tampa Bay during his 14-year career.

17. Yes. The Florida city had the 1974 Jacksonville Sharks in the rival WFL. That franchise changed its name to the Express for the 1975 season, during which time the entire league folded midway through the schedule. In 1984 and 1985, the Jacksonville Bulls played in the USFL, the major spring-time football league.

18. False. His father, Zeke Bratkowski, had a 14-year NFL career as a QB, mainly in the 1950s and 1960s, with the Bears, the LA Rams, and Green Bay.

19. e. But he is Paul Casey Bradley and goes by his middle name when not answering to Gus.

20. b, in 1997.

21. Kicker Mike Hollis.

22. d, in 2006. He also is the team's career leader with 30 lifetime picks. He was released in 2013.

23. Yes, only one. On October 19, 1999, Jacksonville obtained DE Regan Upshaw from Tampa Bay for a future draft choice.
24. False. He was actually born in Germany, although his ancestry is Croatian. He grew up in the Chicago area.
25. Receiver Micah Ross, 2001–03.
26. d. He was born in Lahore, Pakistan, moving to the United States as a teenager. He is a graduate of the University of Illinois (where he did not play football).
27. False. He was a tight end for the Vikings from 1983 to 1988 and for the Steelers from 1989 to 1991.
28. b. Sanya Richards-Ross has won four Olympic gold medals—three in the 4-by-400 relay with the US team in three straight Olympics (2004, 2008, and 2012) and an individual 400 meter gold in London during the 2012 games.
29. No. He was a linebacker at John Carroll University and has 17 years of NFL front-office experience in player personnel.
30. d.

KANSAS CITY CHIEFS

1. Who founded the Chiefs franchise as the Dallas Texans of the AFL in 1959?

2. When did the team move from Dallas to Kansas City?

3. Who coached the Texans/Chiefs for their entire AFL run (1960–69)?

4. Who did KC select with the second-overall choice in the 1988 NFL draft?

5. Which Chiefs defensive stalwart was enshrined in the Pro Football Hall of Fame in Canton in 2013?

6. Which KC receiver broke the one-game NFL receiving yards record with 309 in 1985?

    a. Carlos Carson
    b. Henry Marshall
    c. Stephone Paige
    d. Otis Taylor

7. What Kansas City coach was the second man to hold that job?

   a. Tom Bettis
   b. Marv Levy
   c. John Mackovic
   d. Paul Wiggin

8. Which one of these Chiefs defensive greats is not in the Pro Football Hall of Fame?

   a. Bobby Bell
   b. Buck Buchanan
   c. E.J. Holub
   d. Willie Lanier
   e. Derrick Thomas

9. True or False: Len Dawson was the starter at QB when the franchise began as the Texans in 1960?

10. Where did Marv Levy coach just prior to being hired by the Chiefs in 1978?

11. Which KC back holds the franchise rushing record (most yards in one season)?

   a. Jamaal Charles
   b. Priest Holmes
   c. Larry Johnson
   d. Christian Okoye
   e. Barry Word

12. True or False: Hall of Fame CB Emmitt Thomas was a Chiefs first-round draft choice.

13. Name the father and son who were both Kansas City first-round draft picks, played the same position, and spent their entire NFL careers with the team.

14. What Chief holds the franchise record for most seasons with the club?

15. What player did the Chiefs select with the first overall 2013 NFL draft choice?

16. Where was Gunther Cunningham, KC coach in 1999 and 2000, born?

   a. Detroit
   b. Germany
   c. Hamilton, Canada
   d. Los Angeles
   e. Oregon

17. Who holds the KC franchise record for most receptions in a game, year, and career, as well as most career catches and receiving yards?

18. Which one of these recent Chiefs wasn't drafted in the first three rounds in 2008?

   a. Brandon Albert, T
   b. Jamaal Charles, RB
   c. Glenn Dorsey, DE
   d. Brandon Flowers, CB
   e. Tamba Hali, DE

19. What 1965 Heisman Trophy–winning running back played for the Chiefs for many years, including in their two Super Bowl appearances?

20. Name the 12-time Pro Bowler who never missed a game in his 14-year career, all with Kansas City?

21. Why did RB Joe Delaney, 1981 AFC Rookie of the Year, only play two seasons in the NFL?

22. Who is the most recent Chief to lead the NFL in sacks?

    a. Jared Allen
    b. Tamba Hali
    c. Neil Smith
    d. Derrick Thomas

23. Name the Kansas City QB who holds the single-game team record with 504 passing yards.

    a. Matt Cassel
    b. Len Dawson
    c. Elvis Grbac
    d. Trent Green
    e. Bill Kenney

24. True or False: Jack Steadman was the franchise's original GM.

25. Did owner/founder Lamar Hunt ever play football?

26. Did recent coach Todd Haley play college football?

27. What stadium did the team play in during the first three years in Dallas?

28. What veteran QB did Kansas City trade for prior to the 2013 season?

29. True or False: Bill Kenney (a 1980–88 Chief) is a second-generation NFL QB.

30. Which Chiefs Hall of Famer holds the dubious distinction of having the record for most fumbles in a single game?

KANSAS CITY CHIEFS ANSWERS

1. Lamar Hunt. Hunt, a Hall of Fame inductee, owned the club until his death in December 2006. His family still owns the team, with son Clark Hunt now being the chairman and CEO.
2. 1963. The AFL champions moved from Dallas after three seasons, becoming the Chiefs. (Hunt decided a team called Kansas City Texans would be silly.) They gave up the Dallas area to the Cowboys, relocating to an open city. KC had been without a major pro football team since the KC Cowboys last played in the NFL in 1926.
3. Hank Stram. He stayed with the Chiefs through the NFL merger until 1974, guiding the team to its victory in Super Bowl IV over Minnesota, winning for the AFL in its last year of existence. Stram was admitted to the Hall of Fame in 2003, two years before his death.
4. Neil Smith, defensive end from Nebraska, was their first pick that year. Smith played with the team from 1988 to 1996, earning five consecutive trips to the Pro Bowl during that period.
5. Curley Culp, who was with KC in the AFL and NFL from 1968 to 1974 and was a member of the Super Bowl IV champs.
6. c.
7. d.
8. c. Holub, however, has been in the College Football Hall of Fame since 1976.
9. False. Cotton Davidson was the Texans' starting signal caller in 1960 and 1961. Dawson, who was a backup on the Cleveland Browns in 1960–61, was the QB for the last year in Dallas and for the first of many years in Kansas City.

10. He was head coach of Montreal of the CFL for several years.
11. c. Johnson had 1,789 yards in 2006.
12. False. He was an undrafted free agent in 1966 out of little Bishop College in Dallas.
13. Guards Ed Budde (father, 1963–76) and Brad Budde (son, 1980–86).
14. Punter Jerrel Wilson spent 15 years in KC before playing his final season (1978) with the New England Patriots.
15. Tackle Eric Fisher from Central Michigan.
16. b. He was born in Munich in 1946. He came to the United States as a child and played his college ball for the Oregon Ducks.
17. Tony Gonzalez. The tight end from 1997 to 2008 had 14 catches on January 2, 2004, 102 that season, and 916 during his Chiefs career. He also accumulated 10,940 yards receiving over those 12 years.
18. e. Hall was their first pick in the 2006 draft.
19. Mike Garrett, from USC.
20. Guard Will Shields, 1993–2006.
21. Delaney drowned trying to save drowning children in June 1983 prior to the season. President Reagan presented his family with the Presidential Citizens Medal.
22. a. Allen had 15.5 in 2007. Hali's 14.5 led the AFC in 2010 (not the whole NFL).
23. c. Grbac accomplished this on November 5, 2000.
24. False. Don Rossi was the original GM (of the Texans) until November 1, 1960—not even completing one whole season on the job. Steadman was promoted and remained in that job for 17 years until 1976, when he was promoted to team president.
25. Yes. He was a benchwarmer at Southern Methodist.
26. No. Even though he has the bloodlines because his father, Dick Haley, was an NFL cornerback from 1959 to 1964 and Todd himself was a onetime Steeler ball boy, his college athletic career consisted of being on the golf team.
27. The Cotton Bowl, which was shared with their rivals, the Dallas Cowboys of the NFL.

28. Alex Smith, who had lost his starting job with the 49ers after a 2012 midseason injury.
29. False. His dad, Charlie, played guard for the 49ers (of the rival AAFC) in 1947. (Bill Kenney later became a Missouri state senator, representing KC, after leaving the NFL.)
30. Len Dawson had a record seven fumbles against the Chargers on November 15, 1964.

MIAMI DOLPHINS

1. Which two backs had at least 1,000 yards rushing for Miami's 1972 undefeated, untied team? It was the first time teammates had accomplished that in the same season.

2. Who was the captain of the Dolphins' early-1970s "No-Name Defense"?

3. What three Dolphins offensive stars effectively ended the team's chances for a fourth-straight Super Bowl appearance by signing a future contract, for the 1975 season, with Toronto of the rival WFL in March 1974?

4. Who is the Dolphins Hall of Fame center from the 1980s whose career was cut short by injuries?
   a. Bob DeMarco
   b. Mark Dennard
   c. Tom Goode
   d. Jim Langer
   e. Dwight Stephenson

5. Which Dolphins duo was nicknamed Butch Cassidy and the Sundance Kid (for the popular Paul Newman and Robert Redford movie)?

6. What Miami running back holds the club record for most yards on the ground in a game and for a season? (Hint: The records were set during the same season.)

   a. Kareem Abdul-Jabbar
   b. Larry Csonka
   c. Mercury Morris
   d. Lamar Smith
   e. Ricky Williams

7. What signal caller from Purdue led the squad to three straight Super Bowl appearances (winning the last two), including the perfect 17–0 season in 1972?

8. Was Dan Marino the first QB selected in the 1983 NFL draft?

9. Who did Miami draft in the 12th round in 1966 from Tulsa who went on to become a featured receiver until 1976, including the three straight Super Bowl games?

   a. Frank Jackson
   b. Kent Kramer
   c. Doug Moreau
   d. Karl Noonan
   e. Howard Twilley

10. Was Hall of Fame center Jim Langer a Miami draft choice?

11. Which Miami pass catcher is the franchise career leader in receiving yards with 8,869?

   a. Mark Clayton
   b. Mark Duper
   c. Mark Ingram
   d. Nat Moore
   e. Paul Warfield

12. Who did the Dolphins select the last time they had the NFL's first overall draft choice?

13. Who was the Dolphins first-ever draft choice when the franchise came into being in the 1966 AFL?

    a. Larry Csonka, FB
    b. Jim Grabowski, RB
    c. Bob Griese, QB
    d. Rick Norton, QB

14. Name the first Dolphin to be enshrined in the Pro Football Hall of Fame.

15. Miami traded up to get the third overall choice in the 2013 draft's first round. Who did they select?

16. Which Miami QB holds all of the franchise career, season, and game passing marks—Bob Griese or Dan Marino?

17. Which Dolphin holds the franchise career sacks record?

    a. Trace Armstrong
    b. Doug Betters
    c. Jeff Cross
    d. E.J. Junior
    e. Jason Taylor

18. Match these Miami Hall of Famers with their alma mater:

    1. Nick Buoniconti   **a.** Alabama
    2. Larry Csonka   **b.** Bethune-Cookman
    3. Larry Little   **c.** John Carroll
    4. Dan Marino   **d.** Notre Dame
    5. Don Shula   **e.** Ohio State
    6. Dwight Stephenson   **f.** Pitt
    7. Paul Warfield   **g.** Syracuse

19. Which Dolphin QB holds the franchise's rookie record for passing yards and completions?

   a. Bob Griese
   b. Chad Henne
   c. Dan Marino
   d. Ryan Tannehill

20. Which Miami kicker is the team's all-time scoring leader?

   a. Dan Carpenter
   b. Olindo Mare
   c. Fuad Reveiz
   d. Pete Stoyanovich
   e. Garo Yepremian

21. True or False: Coach Joe Philbin is the son of former Jet great Gerry Philbin.

22. True or False: Reggie Bush is the last Dolphin to lead the NFL in rushing.

23. Name the two 2003 Dolphins who are brothers. One played offense, the other defense.

24. Were the Dolphins the state of Florida's first major pro football team?

25. Name Miami's coach during their AFL years (1966–69).

26. Who was the Dolphins' recent single-year head coach who played college basketball at Indiana for the legendary Bobby Knight?

27. Who tied for the NFL lead with eight interceptions along with Steeler Mike Wagner in 1973?

a. Dick Anderson
b. Tim Foley
c. Curtis Johnson
d. Jake Scott

28. Which member of the Dolphins' No-Name (Super Bowl) Defense from Georgia was both the 1968 Outland Trophy winner and an Academic All-American in 1968?

29. What Dolphins 1981 first-round draft pick running back from Oklahoma didn't play for the team until 1983 and died in an offseason auto accident in June 1984?

30. Who was the last Miami back to lead the league in rushing?

MIAMI DOLPHINS ANSWERS

1. Larry Csonka and Mercury Morris. Csonka had 1,117 while Morris had 1,000 even.
2. Nick Buoniconti, linebacker.
3. Fullback Larry Csonka, halfback Jim Kiick, and receiver Paul Warfield. The trio left Miami for the WFL club, which actually played in Memphis, abandoning Toronto before beginning its first training camp.
4. e.
5. Larry Csonka (Butch) and Jim Kiick (Sundance).
6. e. Williams led the NFL with 1,853 yards in 2002 with a high of 228 yards on December 1 of that season.
7. Bob Griese.
8. No. Miami picked him in the first round with the 27th overall selection. Five QBs (John Elway, Jim Kelly, Ken O'Brien, Todd Blackledge, and Tony Eason) all went ahead of him.
9. e.
10. No. He signed as a free agent in 1970 after being an undrafted tryout player cut by the Steelers in training camp.
11. b.
12. Jake Long, tackle, in 2008.

13. b. Grabowski signed with Green Bay, the team that selected him with its first-round pick that year.
14. Paul Warfield in 1983.
15. Dion Jordan, defensive end from the Oregon Ducks.
16. Marino, who broke all of Griese's team records with the exception of tying Griese's one-game TD mark with six.
17. e. Taylor had 124 sacks.
18. 1. d; 2. g; 3. b; 4. f; 5. c; 6. a; 7. e.
19. d, in 2012.
20. b. Mare had 1,048 points in his ten years with the club (1997–2006).
21. False. They're not related (and Joe isn't related to talk show host Regis Philbin either).
22. False. Bush never led the league. The last man to do so was Ricky Williams in 2002.
23. FB Obafemi Ayanbadejo and LB Brendon Ayanbadejo.
24. No. The Miami Seahawks of the first-year AAFC in 1946 were a weak team with an even weaker box office. They were dissolved soon after the season ended.
25. George Wilson, who had previously coached the Detroit Lions several years before.
26. Cam Cameron.
27. a. Anderson was a Pro Bowl safety from Colorado whose brother Bobby (RB) and son Blake (WR) also played for that university. Bobby also played in the NFL.
28. Bill Stanfill, DT.
29. David Overstreet, who signed with Montreal of the CFL in 1981 after a contract dispute with Miami, playing in Canada for two years.
30. Ricky Williams in 2002, when he set the club record with 1,853 yards.

MINNESOTA VIKINGS

1. QB Fran Tarkenton was traded for the same player twice, once when the Vikings traded him away and again when they reacquired him. Who is that player?

2. RB D.J. Dozier was a two-sport major leaguer. What was his other sport?

3. Minnesota's original coach in 1961 was Norm Van Brocklin. What was his prior coaching background?

4. Bud Grant followed Van Brocklin as the Vikings' second coach. What was his coaching background?

5. Had Grant ever played in the NFL?

6. Defensive line star Carl Eller hails from what university?
   a. Hamline
   b. Minnesota
   c. St. Thomas
   d. Winston-Salem State
   e. Wisconsin

7. What was Alan Page, Hall of Fame defensive tackle, known for after football?

8. Who were the other members of the Purple People Eaters (the team's defensive front four in the early glory years), along with Page?

9. Match these starting QBs with their alma mater:

   1. Daunte Culpepper   a. California
   2. Joe Kapp   b. Central Florida
   3. Tommy Kramer   c. Florida State
   4. Bob Lee   d. Georgia
   5. Warren Moon   e. Pacific
   6. Christian Ponder   f. Rice
   7. Fran Tarkenton   g. Washington

10. What Viking led the NFC with 1,521 yards rushing in 2000 then retired after the season?

11. True or False: The Vikings had brothers playing for them in 1998 and 1999.

12. What is Amp Lee's, Vikings running back from 1996 to 1998, actual first name?

   a. Ammon
   b. Ampere
   c. Ampton
   d. Anthonia
   e. Anthony

13. Who is the most recent Viking to win NFL MVP?

14. Who did Minnesota select with their first pick in the 1961 NFL draft?

a. Rip Hawkins, LB
b. Tommy Mason, HB
c. Mike Mercer, K
d. Ed Sharockman, DB
e. Fran Tarkenton, QB

15. Which kicker is Minnesota's all-time scoring leader?

a. Morten Andersen
b. Gary Anderson
c. Fred Cox
d. Rich Karlis
e. Ryan Longwell

16. Which one of these players was not one of the Vikings' three 2013 first-round draft picks?

a. Sharrif Floyd, DT
b. Cordarrelle Patterson, WR
c. Xavier Rhodes, CB
d. Manti Te'o, LB

17. True or False: The expansion Vikings lost their first eight games in 1961.

18. Which QB directed Minnesota to the 1969 NFL championship—the last one prior to the NFL/AFL merger going into effect? (They lost Super Bowl IV to the Chiefs.)

a. Bob Berry
b. Joe Kapp
c. Tommy Kramer
d. Norm Snead
e. Fran Tarkenton

19. Name the NFL's career interception leader. (Hint: He also holds the Minnesota lifetime record with 53 picks.)

20. True or False: Center Mick Tingelhoff, who played from 1962 to 1978, all with the Vikings, and was named to seven straight All-Pro teams, is in the Hall of Fame.

21. What two players on the 1961 expansion team (not including coach Van Brocklin) were eventually elected to the Hall of Fame?

22. Does coach Leslie Frazier have a Super Bowl ring as a player?

23. Who was the new coach in 1984, replacing the retiring Bud Grant?

24. True or False: Defensive lineman John Randle has a brother who also played for the Vikings.

25. Who was the Vikings' first GM?
  a. Jim Finks
  b. Mike Lynn
  c. Bert Rose
  d. Max Winter

26. Name the Vikings running back who competed for the United States in the two-man bobsled event in the 1992 Winter Olympics.

27. Bud Grant was a two-sport major leaguer. What was his other sport?

28. Who was the Vikings' sixth-round draft pick center, considered one of the all-time draft finds, who made six Pro Bowls in 11 years in Minnesota? (Hint: He just retired in 2013 after winning a Super Bowl as a member of the Ravens.)

29. Which QB was drafted in the eighth round by Minnesota in 1981, eventually became the starter, and was named to the Pro Bowl as a Viking in 1988?

30. Name the Viking receiver who won 1963 NFL Rookie of the Year.

MINNESOTA VIKINGS ANSWERS

1. Receiver Bob Grim was part of the package from the NY Giants for Tark in 1967 (as a second-round draft choice picked by the Vikings), and to New York in 1972. Grim went back to Minnesota in 1976, where he and Fran played together for two seasons.
2. Baseball. He was an outfielder with the New York Mets in 1992.
3. He had none. He had retired prior to the season after having quarterbacked Philadelphia to the 1960 NFL championship and won the NFL MVP.
4. He had been coach of the Winnipeg Blue Bombers of the CFL, winning several CFL Grey Cup championships.
5. Yes. He was a two-way end for the Eagles in 1951–52.
6. b. Eller came from the Vikings' backyard. Nowadays, that university's football defensive player of the year receives the annual Carl Eller Award.
7. He is currently a Minnesota Supreme Court judge, serving in that capacity since 1992.
8. Defensive ends Carl Eller and Jim Marshall, and Gary Larsen at the other tackle.
9. 1. b; 2. a; 3. f; 4. e; 5. g; 6. c; 7. d.
10. Robert Smith.
11. True. Star receiver Randy Moss and his half-brother, offensive lineman Eric Moss, were teammates for those two seasons.
12. d.
13. Adrian Peterson in 2012. Peterson had a league leading 2,097 rushing yards (second all-time for a single season) after having his 2011 season cut short, requiring knee surgery.

14. b.
15. c. Cox scored 1,365 points, playing for the Vikes his entire career (1963–77). Morten Andersen is the NFL's career scoring leader, but he only spent one year with the team.
16. d.
17. False. The club won its first-ever game, crushing the Chicago Bears at home, 37–13. Then they lost seven straight games before they won again. They finished 3–11 that year.
18. b.
19. Paul Krause with 81 interceptions. He spent 12 of his 16 NFL seasons with the Vikings.
20. False. He probably should be.
21. Rookie QB Fran Tarkenton and HB Hugh McElhenny, the oldest man on the team.
22. Yes. He was a starting cornerback for the Super Bowl XX–winning Bears. He also has a second ring as an assistant coach with Indianapolis in Super Bowl XLI.
23. Les Steckel, an assistant coach, was elevated to head coach for 1984. He was fired after a 3–13 record and replaced by Bud Grant in 1985.
24. False. His brother Ervin Randle, a linebacker, played for Tampa Bay and Kansas City.
25. c. Rose was hired in August 1960 as the first GM of the team, which was to begin play in the fall of 1961. He is credited with choosing the Vikings' team name. Winter was the original owner.
26. Herschel Walker. He left the team as a free agent before the 1992 season, signing with Philadelphia.
27. Basketball. He was on NBA Championship teams with the Minneapolis Lakers in the early 1950s.
28. Matt Birk.
29. Wade Wilson, from little East Texas State. He played 11 years on the Vikings and 19 NFL seasons altogether (up to age 40).
30. Paul Flatley.

NEW ENGLAND PATRIOTS

1. What 2013 Hall of Fame inductee won the 1994 NFL Coach of the Year award with the Patriots?

2. What Patriots 1973 first-round draft choice spent his entire NFL career with them and is a Hall of Famer considered one of the all-time great guards?

3. Name the Boston Patriots' second coach (1961–68) who had previously coached his alma mater (Boston College) and had been a Rams and Bears running back from 1946 to 1948?
   a. Ron Erhardt
   b. Mike Holovak
   c. John Mazur
   d. Clive Rush
   e. Lou Saban

4. What Pats fullback from Syracuse University led the AFL in rushing yards in both 1965 and 1966?

    a. Joe Bellino
    b. Ron Burton
    c. J.D. Garrett
    d. Jim Nance

5. To whom is star quarterback Tom Brady married?

    a. Giselle Bundchen
    b. Beyoncé Knowles
    c. Gwyneth Paltrow
    d. Eve Plumb
    e. Rihanna

6. What 1970 Heisman Trophy–winning QB was named 1971 NFL Rookie of the Year for the Patriots?

7. Who currently owns the Patriots?

    a. Victor Kiam
    b. Robert Kraft
    c. James Orthwein
    d. Billy Sullivan

8. Which Patriot took 1985 AFC Defensive Player of the Year honors from UPI?

    a. Julius Adams
    b. Raymond Clayborn
    c. Steve Nelson
    d. Andre Tippett

9. By what nickname is nose tackle Raymond Hamilton known?

10. Match these Patriots with their alma mater:

1. Drew Bledsoe	a. Alabama
2. Tom Brady	b. Arizona State
3. Irving Fryar	c. Iowa
4. Rob Gronkowski	d. Miami
5. John Hannah	e. Michigan
6. Curtis Martin	f. Nebraska
7. Willie McGinest	g. Pitt
8. Jim Plunkett	h. Stanford
9. Andre Tippett	i. Texas Tech
10. Wes Welker	j. USC
11. Vince Wilfork	k. Washington State

11. Who holds the single-season New England rushing record?

   a. Tony Collins
   b. Sam "Bam" Cunningham
   c. Corey Dillon
   d. BenJarvus Green-Ellis
   e. Jim Nance

12. Which Hall of Fame defensive star holds the franchise's career sacks record?

   a. Julius Adams
   b. Nick Buoniconti
   c. Kenneth Sims
   d. Andre Tippett

13. Which Patriot led the AFL in scoring for five out of six seasons?

14. What year did the Patriots first get into the playoffs?

   a. 1960
   b. 1963
   c. 1976
   d. 1978
   e. 1985

15. Tom Brady set the NFL's record for touchdown passes in 2007. How many did he throw?

a. 40
b. 43
c. 49
d. 50
e. 52

16. Who was the NFL Defensive Rookie of the Year in 1976?

a. Richard Bishop
b. Tim Fox
c. Mike Haynes
d. Dave Tipton

17. Which New England stalwart is the NFL's career leader in playoff sacks with 16?

a. Tedy Bruschi
b. Willie McGinest
c. Junior Seau
d. Richard Seymour
e. Andre Tippett

18. Match the New England receiver with his team record:

1. Troy Brown   a. 10,352 career receiving yards
2. Stanley Morgan   b. 123 receptions in a season
3. Randy Moss   c. 557 career catches
4. Wes Welker   d. most TDs in one season (23)

19. Which Patriots defensive tackle (1961–71) is on the Pro Football Hall of Fame's All-Time AFL team?

a. Houston Antwine
b. Bob Dee
c. Larry Eisenhauer
d. Jim "Earthquake" Hunt
e. Jess Richardson

20. When did the Patriots move to Foxboro, Massachusetts, and change their name to New England?

21. Name the Patriots receiver who became a quadriplegic after a spinal cord injury caused by being tackled by Oakland's Jack Tatum in an August 1978 preseason game?

22. Who was the Patriots' head coach immediately before the club hired Bill Belichick?

  a. Pete Carroll
  b. Dick MacPherson
  c. Bill Parcells
  d. Rod Rust

23. Adam Vinatieri, the Pats' former kicker, is the NFL's career playoff scoring leader with 177 points. What pro team did he play for prior to coming to the club in 1996?

24. True or False: The Boston Patriots were the first NFL team from Boston.

25. What coach was suspended for the team's final regular season game in 1978 before being allowed to coach in the playoffs, and why was he suspended?

  a. Hank Bullough
  b. Ron Erhardt
  c. Chuck Fairbanks
  d. Ron Meyer

26. Who was the 1985 Outland Trophy recipient from nearby Boston College whose entire NFL career consisted of two years as a Pats defensive lineman?

27. Which 1959 Heisman Trophy winner from Navy didn't join the team until 1965 because of military commitment even though he was drafted by the club in 1961?

28. What 1981 Lombardi Award defensive tackle from the Texas Longhorns did the Patriots switch to defensive end as an NFL rookie?

   a. Julius Adams
   b. Don Blackmon
   c. Kenneth Sims
   d. Lester Williams

29. TE Rob Gronkowski has how many brothers who have played in the NFL?

   a. 0
   b. 1
   c. 2
   d. 5

30. Who holds the team record for the longest TD?

NEW ENGLAND PATRIOTS ANSWERS

1. Bill Parcells.
2. John Hannah.
3. b.
4. d.
5. a. Brady is married to model Giselle Bundchen.
6. Jim Plunkett.
7. b.
8. d.
9. Sugar Bear.
10. 1. k; 2. e; 3. f; 4. b; 5. a; 6. g; 7. j; 8. h; 9. c; 10. i; 11. d.
11. c. He had 1,635 yards in 2004.

12. d. He has an even 100.
13. Gino Cappelletti. He was both an end who scored TDs and the Pats' place kicker, leading the league in points in 1961 and from 1963 through 1966.
14. b. The Boston Patriots tied for the AFL Eastern Division lead at the end of the regular season. They had to beat Buffalo in a special division playoff 26–8, then lost to San Diego 51–10 in the AFL championship game.
15. d.
16. c.
17. b.
18. 1. c; 2. a; 3. d; 4. b.
19. a.
20. In 1971. It was the team's second year in the NFL after the AFL-NFL merger took effect in 1970.
21. Darryl Stingley. The NFL legislated the first of several rule changes protecting offensive players from vicious and violent hits as a result of this tragic occurrence.
22. a. Carroll, the current Seahawks coach, was the Pats' coach from 1996 to 1999. He later became USC coach, winning an NCAA national championship there.
23. He was on the Amsterdam Admirals of NFL Europe and was signed as an undrafted free agent by New England.
24. False. The first NFL team was the Boston Bulldogs in 1929. There also had been a team with that same name in the original AFL, a rival league, in 1926. Both of those teams went out of business after only one year. The Boston Braves, who later changed their name to Redskins, played in the NFL from 1932 to 1936 before moving to Washington permanently in 1937, and the Boston Yanks played in the league from 1944 to 1948 before moving to New York City in 1949 (and going out of business a few years later).
25. c. Owner Billy Sullivan suspended Fairbanks for breach of contract after the announcement that Fairbanks would become coach of the University of Colorado in 1979. Bullough and Erhardt served as co-coaches for the team's last game loss, but Fairbanks was allowed to coach the playoff game (which New England lost). He did leave for

Colorado in 1979, and Erhardt became the new head coach that year.

26. Mike Ruth. Injuries curtailed a promising career.

27. Joe Bellino, an AFL Patriot running back from 1965 to 1967.

28. c.

29. c. His brothers Chris and Dan have also played in the league recently.

30. Ellis Hobbs had a 108-yard kickoff return TD versus the Jets on opening day of the Patriots' 2007 season, September 9.

NEW ORLEANS SAINTS

1. Who is the most recent Saint to be inducted into the Pro Football Hall of Fame?

2. Did Ricky Williams play professional sports prior to being the Saints' first-round pick from the University of Texas in 1999?

3. Which Saints coach's pro playing career consists of just three games as a 1987 Chicago replacement QB during an NFL strike?

4. Which two Saints head coaches from 1985 are father and son?

5. Who is the Saints linebacker elected to the Hall of Fame in 2010?

6. Name the Louisiana native of Cajun heritage and former star QB from the rival USFL who led the Saints to their first ever playoff berth in 1987?

7. What 1980 Heisman winner was named 1981 NFL Rookie of the Year after leading the league in rushing yardage?

8. Where had Jim Mora Sr. coached immediately prior to being hired by the Saints?

9. Who is the 5'9" linebacker who was cut in training camp by Cleveland and Toronto of the CFL before finally making the cut in the USFL, then playing in four Pro Bowls during his years with the Saints (1986–94)?

   a. Vaughn Johnson
   b. Sam Mills
   c. Pat Swilling
   d. Dennis "Dirt" Winston

10. What is the Saints' record in playoff games with Archie Manning at QB?

11. Which Saint led the NFL with 17 sacks in 1991?

   a. Rickey Jackson
   b. Sam Mills
   c. Pat Swilling
   d. Renaldo Turnbull
   e. Frank Warren

12. Which back holds the New Orleans career record for rushing yardage?

   a. Reggie Bush
   b. Earl Campbell
   c. Deuce McAllister
   d. George Rogers
   e. Ricky Williams

13. What Hall of Fame player was the Saints' first coach in 1967?

14. Which kicker leads New Orleans in career scoring and is the NFL's all-time scoring leader as well?

   a. Morten Andersen
   b. John Carney
   c. Tom Dempsey
   d. Jon Kasay

15. Who was the Saints' interim coach for the first six games of 2012?

   a. Jim Has
   b. Aaron Kromer
   c. Sean Payton
   d. Steve Spagnuolo
   e. Joe Vitt

16. True or False: The Saints have never had an overtime play-off game.

17. Who was not suspended by the NFL as a result of the 2012 Bountygate investigation?

   a. Owner Tom Benson
   b. GM Mickey Loomis
   c. Coach Sean Payton
   d. LB Jonathan Vilma
   e. DC Gregg Williams

18. Which current Saints back has a father who played in the NFL?

19. Who is the Saints' career leader in receptions and reception yards?

   a. Wes Chand

   b. Marques Colston

   c. Jimmy Graham

   d. Joe Horn

   e. Eric Martin

20. New Orleans was an NFL expansion team in 1967. When did they have their first winning season?

   a. 1969

   b. 1977

   c. 1979

   d. 1988

   e. 1991

21. Match these Saints with their alma mater:

1. Drew Brees	**a.** Alabama
2. Marques Colston	**b.** Hofstra
3. Mark Ingram	**c.** Kansas State
4. Rickey Jackson	**d.** Louisiana Tech
5. Archie Manning	**e.** Miami
6. Deuce McAllister	**f.** Ole Miss
7. Tommy Myers	**g.** Pittsburgh
8. Willie Roaf	**h.** Purdue
9. George Rogers	**i.** South Carolina
10. Darren Sproles	**j.** Syracuse

22. Who is the Saints' winningest coach?

   a. Mike Ditka

   b. Jim Haslett

   c. Jim Mora

   d. Sean Payton

   e. Hank Stram

23. Which Saint set a new NFL record for all-purpose yardage in 2011? (Note: This includes rushing, receiving, and kick-off and punt returns.)

24. Where did receiver Joe Horn play his college ball?

25. Which Saint tied for the league lead with ten interceptions in 1967, the club's expansion year?

    a. Bo Burris
    b. Ross Fichtner
    c. Elbert Kimbrough
    d. Obert Logan
    e. Dave Whitsell

26. How did the Saints acquire defensive lineman Bruce Clark, the 1978 Lombardi Award recipient from Penn State?

27. Which Saints coach won the 1953 Outland Trophy as an Oklahoma University guard but never played pro football?

    a. Ernie Hefferle
    b. John North
    c. J.D. Roberts
    d. Hank Stram

28. Who was the BYU defensive tackle whom the Saints selected with the 11th overall pick in the 1987 NFL draft and is considered one of the all-time NFL draft busts?

29. Conversely, what Saints 2006 seventh-round pick receiver is considered one the NFL draft's hidden gems?

30. The Saints used their 2013 first-round pick on the first safety selected that year—who is he?

NEW ORLEANS SAINTS ANSWERS

1. Willie Roaf, star offensive tackle from 1993 to 2001, was named to the Hall in 2012.
2. Yes. He played four seasons of minor league baseball in the Philadelphia Phillies' farm system from 1995 to 1998 in the outfield.
3. Sean Payton.
4. Bum Phillips resigned after 12 games and was replaced by his son Wade Phillips, who went 1–3 the rest of the way.
5. Rickey Jackson (1981–93).
6. Bobby Hebert.
7. George Rogers (1,674 yards).
8. The Baltimore Stars of the rival USFL.
9. b.
10. 0–0. They never made the playoffs during Archie's tenure. He is the father of current QBs Peyton and Eli Manning, who have three Super Bowl wins between them.
11. c.
12. c. McAllister racked up 6,096 yards during his nine-year Saints career.
13. Tom Fears.
14. a. Andersen spent the first 13 of his 25 NFL seasons with the Saints.
15. b.
16. False. They beat Minnesota 31–28 in OT in the NFC Championship game on January 24, 2010, on their way to their only Super Bowl.
17. a. The NFL suspensions for the alleged cash bounty to defensive players for causing opponents injuries affected coaches, players, assistants, and executives. Owner Benson was not included.
18. Mark Ingram Jr. His father, Mark Sr., spent ten years in the league as a receiver (1987–96).
19. e.
20. d. They didn't have a winning year until their 22nd year in the league, when they went 12–3 and earned a wild-card playoff berth. They did achieve a .500 record (8–8) in 1979.
21. 1. h; 2. b; 3. a; 4. g; 5. f; 6. e; 7. j; 8. d; 9. i; 10. c.

22. c. Mora won 93 games, more than Payton, who won a Super Bowl, or Ditka and Stram, who are in the Hall of Fame.
23. Darren Sproles with 2,696.
24. Horn played at Itawamba Community College, a two-year school in Mississippi. He was drafted in the fifth round by Kansas City in 1996 after spending a year in Canadian football with Shreveport and Memphis when the CFL featured American-based teams. He came to the Saints in 2000, remaining for a seven-year stretch.
25. e. The 31-year-old former Bear Whitsell still has the team record for picks in a season.
26. Clark signed as a free agent with the Saints in 1982 after he spent the first two years of his pro career with Toronto of the CFL. He was the fourth overall pick in the draft by Green Bay in 1980 but signed to play in Canada instead.
27. c.
28. Shawn Knight, who had no sacks in his three years in the NFL, only one of which was with the Saints.
29. Marques Colston, out of Hofstra, is in his eighth year with the team as one of Drew Brees's favorite targets.
30. Kenny Vaccaro from the University of Texas Longhorns.

NEW YORK GIANTS

1. He played his entire NFL career with the Giants, after leading the Canadian Football League Big Four division in rushing for Montreal in 1954. Who is this running back, known as Big Red, who later coached the Giants?

2. Who is the Giants defensive end who was a frequent All-Pro selection and is now the cohost of a leading daytime TV talk show?

3. Which quarterback took over for the injured Phil Simms late in the 1990 season and led the Giants to victory in Super Bowl XXV?

   a. Scott Brunner
   b. Kerry Collins
   c. Jeff Hostetler
   d. Jeff Rutledge

4. When did the Giants win their first NFL championship?

   a. 1925
   b. 1927
   c. 1938
   d. 1941

5. How many Giants were inducted with the initial Pro Football Hall of Fame class in 1963?

6. True or False: The Giants drafted Eli Manning as the first overall choice in 2004?

7. True or False: Tom Coughlin has been the Giants head coach longer than anyone else.

8. Who was the last Giant to win Rookie of the Year?

   a. Tiki Barber
   b. Victor Cruz
   c. Eli Manning
   d. Lawrence Taylor

9. Actress Kate Mara (*Brokeback Mountain*, *24*) is the granddaughter of the late Giants owner Wellington Mara. Who is her maternal great grandfather?

10. Name the 2012 Giant rookie who was born in Germany.

11. Which QB started the most games for the Giants in both 1997 and 1998?

   a. Dave Brown
   b. Kerry Collins
   c. Kent Graham
   d. Danny Kanell
   e. Phil Simms

12. Who was the Giants punter who was acquired after the demise of the rival USFL in 1985?

13. Which Giants GM was the architect of the team that had victories in Super Bowls XXI and XXV?

a. Ernie Accorsi
b. Jerry Reese
c. Andy Robustelli
d. Bob Tisch
e. George Young

14. Which Giant was the first in franchise history to surpass 1,000 yards rushing in a season?

a. Tucker Frederickson
b. Frank Gifford
c. Ron Johnson
d. Joe Morris
e. Mel Triplett

15. Who is the Giants' all-time sacks leader?

a. Carl Banks
b. Leonard Marshall
c. Michael Strahan
d. Lawrence Taylor
e. Brad Van Pelt

16. Name the Giants player who starred on TV's *The Bachelor* in the off-season during his playing career.

17. Who was the Giants long snapper whose bad snap resulted in a botched field goal attempt that might have won a January 2003 playoff game against the 49ers?

a. Zak DeOssie
b. Trey Junkin
c. Glen Parker
d. Omar Smith
e. Dusty Ziegler

18. Name the recent Giants running back trio known as "Earth, Wind, and Fire."

19. Which two longtime Giants star QBs hail from "Ole Miss" (University of Mississippi)?

20. Match these Giants Hall of Famers with their alma mater:

1. Roosevelt Brown	**a.** Arnold College (CT)
2. Harry Carson	**b.** Fordham
3. Mel Hein	**c.** Iowa
4. Sam Huff	**d.** LSU
5. Wellington Mara	**e.** Morgan State
6. Steve Owen	**f.** North Carolina
7. Bill Parcells	**g.** NYU
8. Andy Robustelli	**h.** Phillips (OK)
9. Ken Strong	**i.** South Carolina State
10. Lawrence Taylor	**j.** Washington State
11. Y.A. Tittle	**k.** West Virginia
12. Emlen Tunnell	**l.** Wichita State

21. DE George Martin played his entire 14-year career with New York and was defensive captain of the Super Bowl XXI champs. In what round did the Giants select him in the 1975 NFL draft?

a. 1st
b. 2nd
c. 4th
d. 7th
e. 11th

22. Kyle Rote, 11-year Giants receiver from SMU and a member of the College Football Hall of Fame, had a son who played pro sports. For what sport was Kyle Rote Jr. known?

23. Hall of Famer Frank Gifford played for the Giants from 1952 to 1965 but is perhaps better known for what he did after leaving the playing field. What did Giff do in his second career?

24. Match the former Giant with his nickname:

1. Ottis Anderson		**a.** Bookie
2. Morris Badgro		**b.** Butch
3. Treva Bolin		**c.** Hap
4. John Elliott		**d.** Hinkey
5. Denver Gibson		**e.** Jumbo
6. Henry Haines		**f.** O.J.
7. Thomas Johnson		**g.** Pepper
8. Alphonse Leemans		**h.** Red
9. Carl Lockhart		**i.** Rocky
10. Francis Moran		**j.** Spider
11. Ralph Thompson		**k.** Tuffy

25. Name the Giants placekicker who holds the club record with six field goals in a single game:

a. Don Chandler
b. Joe Danelo
c. Ali Haji-Sheikh
d. Pat Summerall
e. Lawrence Tynes

26. Which Giants coach played his high school football for Blanton Collier and college ball for Woody Hayes, then earned his early coaching credentials as a college assistant for both of them at different times?

a. Bill Arnsparger
b. Ray Handley
c. John McVay
d. Allie Sherman

27. Who was the Giant end from 1937 to 1947 (missing some time during World War II) and coach from 1948 to 1953 for Wagner College on Staten Island who went on to coach the Giants from 1954 to 1960? (Note: He also found time to serve as an Arkansas state legislator.)

28. Where was early NFL star end Bob "Nasty" Nash, a 1925 original Giant, born?

  a. Akron
  b. Buffalo
  c. Ireland
  d. New Jersey
  e. Rochester

29. True or False: Jim Fassel, coach of the Giants in Super Bowl XXXV, played QB in the NFL.

30. Name the promising Giants defensive lineman who was killed in an auto accident during the squad's training camp in June 1979.

NEW YORK GIANTS ANSWERS

1. Alex Webster. He played for New York from 1955 to 1964 and was head coach from 1969 to 1973.
2. Michael Strahan (ABC's *Live with Kelly and Michael*).
3. c. Hostetler beat out Simms in training camp the next season to stay as the starter but was likewise injured late in the season.
4. b. The Giants reached the pinnacle in only their third year of existence.
5. Four. Mel Hein, Cal Hubbard, owner Tim Mara, and Jim Thorpe. Hubbard also played for Green Bay (and is better known for his years as a baseball umpire), while Thorpe was an aging star who only played for New York in its initial 1925 NFL season.
6. False. While Manning was the first pick in the 2004 NFL draft, he was selected by San Diego, who traded him later that day to the Giants for quarterback Philip Rivers (the Giants' first pick) and three other draft picks.
7. False. Coughlin is second on the list after completing his ninth season with the club in 2012. He has a very long way

to go to catch Hall of Famer Steve Owen, who coached the team for more than 23 seasons from late 1930 through 1953.

8. d. Taylor won Defensive Rookie of the Year in 1981 and is the only Giant to win since the award started in 1957.

9. The late Art Rooney, founder of the Pittsburgh Steelers.

10. Markus Kuhn, a defensive tackle who was their seventh-round draft pick.

11. d. Kanell started ten games in each of those seasons. (Brown started six in 1997, while Graham started six in 1998.)

12. Sean Landeta. Landeta was a Giant for nine years, including the 1986 and 1990 NFL champion squads. He played for the Philadelphia/Baltimore Stars during the USFL's three-year existence.

13. e. Young constructed the 1990 and 1994 teams during his years as GM from 1979 to 1987. He was voted the NFL's Executive of the Year five times during that period.

14. c. Johnson piled up 1,027 yards in 1970, finishing second in the league behind Washington's Larry Brown.

15. c. Strahan tops the list with 141.5 lifetime sacks. He also had an NFL record single-season mark of 22.5 in 2001.

16. Jesse Palmer. Palmer, a backup QB during his NFL career, is now on TV as an ABC and ESPN announcer.

17. b. It was Junkin's final game of a 19-year NFL career and his only game with New York.

18. Brandon Jacobs (Earth), Ahmad Bradshaw (Wind), and Derrick Ward (Fire). The trio's nickname was coined by their teammate Justin Tuck, a defensive lineman.

19. Charlie Conerly and current signal caller Eli Manning.

20. 1.e; 2. i; 3. j; 4. k; 5. b; 6. h; 7. l; 8. a; 9. g; 10. f; 11. d; 12. c.

21. e. New York waited until the 11th round to take Martin out of the University of Oregon with the 262nd overall pick. Nowadays, the draft only goes to round seven.

22. Soccer. Kyle Jr. was a forward in the North American Soccer League for eight years with Dallas and Houston from 1972 to 1979. He also played for the US national team and is enshrined in the National Soccer Hall of Fame. Kyle Sr. had a

cousin, QB Tobin Rote, who was his contemporary, playing in the NFL, CFL, and AFL during the 1950s and 1960s.

23. Gifford was a mainstay announcer on ABC's *Monday Night Football* from 1971 to 1997, twice as long as his playing career.

24. 1. f; 2. h; 3. a; 4. e; 5. b; 6. d; 7. g; 8. k; 9. j; 10. c; 11. i.

25. b. Danelo booted six three-pointers through the uprights at Seattle on October 18, 1981, tying a then NFL record (since broken).

26. a.

27. Jim Lee Howell.

28. c. Nash hailed from Ireland. He played at Rutgers and was a star of the NFL's formative years (1920–24) with Akron, the Buffalo All-Americans, and Rochester before spending his final pro season with the Giants in 1925.

29. False. Fassel did, however, play QB for the Hawaiians in the short-lived rival WFL in 1974 and 1975. He was the seventh-round draft pick of the Bears in 1972 but was cut in training camp by Chicago as well as Miami that preseason.

30. Troy Archer, who was their first-round draft pick in 1976 from the University of Colorado and a three-year starter at defensive tackle.

NEW YORK JETS

1. Who did the Jets draft with the first overall choice in 1996?

2. Who is the 1963 linebacker who became the team's head coach over a decade later?

3. Was Joe Namath the reigning Heisman Trophy winner when the Jets picked him in the first round of the 1965 AFL draft?

4. Who is the Jets career rushing yardage leader who had seven consecutive 1,000-yard seasons as a Jet (and ten in a row overall)?

5. What Football Hall of Fame inductee was the initial coach of the franchise in the AFL in 1960?

6. Name the four Jets defensive linemen known collectively as the NY Sack Exchange in the 1980s.

7. Who is the Jets' all-time career leader in pass receptions, reception yards, and TDs?

    a. Santonio Holmes
    b. Don Maynard
    c. Al Toon
    d. JoJo Townsell
    e. Wesley Walker

8. True or False: Buddy Ryan, the father of current coach Rex Ryan, was also the Jets head coach at one time.

9. Name the NY Titan who led the AFL in receiving yardage in 1962 (with 1,130), then had an even better year in 1963 after being traded to Oakland.

10. Who was the first-ever QB to surpass 4,000 yards passing in a season?

11. True or False: Jets runner Marion Barber (1982–88) had relatives who also played in the NFL.

12. Which Jet running back has the team rushing record with 210 yards in a game?

    a. Emerson Boozer
    b. Thomas Jones
    c. Curtis Martin
    d. John Riggins
    e. Matt Snell

13. Name the Jet who played more seasons than any other in franchise history and leads the team in lifetime scoring.

14. Which Jets coach has the most wins?

a. Herm Edwards
b. Weeb Ewbank
c. Walt Michaels
d. Bill Parcells
e. Joe Walton

15. Mark Sanchez led the Jets to the AFC Conference finals in 2009 as a rookie and in 2010 as a second-year man. Who was the Jets' QB in 2008?

16. True or False: Recent Jets fullback Tony Richardson and cornerback Ray Mickens are products of NFL Europe.

17. The Jets' green-and-white team colors are well known. What were the jersey colors when the team was called the Titans from 1960 to 1962?

18. Name the College Football Hall of Fame coach who quit with a game to go in 1976, his only NFL season?

19. True or False: Linebacker Larry Grantham spent his entire pro career with the franchise.

20. What is Super Bowl III punter Curley Johnson's first name?

21. Name the Jets punter who made the Pro Bowl in 1999 but originally came into the league as a quarterback.

22. Who holds the team record with 12 interceptions in a season?
a. Bill Baird
b. Ty Law
c. Dainard Paulson
d. Darrelle Revis
e. Johnny Sample

23. Who led the AFL with 2,147 all-purpose yards in 1962? (Note: This includes rushing, receiving, kickoff returns, and punt returns.)

   a. Dick Christy
   b. Thurlow Cooper
   c. Bill Mathis
   d. Don Maynard
   e. Bill Shockley

24. What starting QB for the NY Titans led the AFL in TD passes during the league's first year (1960)?

25. What player was the first on-field fatality in AFL history?

26. Where was 1970s defensive back Chris Farasopoulos born?

27. Which Jets linebacker (1993–2003) from Florida State made All-Pro in 2000 after winning both the Lombardi and Butkus awards in 1992?

28. Which player spent his entire career with the team (1960–69) in the AFL but retired before the Jets joined the NFL in 1970?

   a. Bill Baird
   b. Jim Hudson
   c. Bill Mathis
   d. Don Maynard
   e. Joe Namath

29. Who is the Brooklyn-born 1957 Maxwell Award winner from Navy (and College Hall of Famer) who was an original Titan defensive end in 1960–61?

a. Larry Baker
b. Roger Ellis
c. Nick Mumley
d. Bob Reifsnyder

30. Who was the Jets' 12th-round draft pick in 1967 who spent his entire 15-year career (1967–81) at guard with the team?

NEW YORK JETS ANSWERS

1. Keyshawn Johnson, receiver from USC.
2. Walt Michaels.
3. No. The Heisman winner for 1964 was QB John Huarte, the Jets' second-round pick that year. Huarte backed up Namath for several years but never got into a game.
4. Curtis Martin, with 10,302 yards.
5. Sammy Baugh, famed Redskins QB and the coach of little Hardin–Simmons College (TX), was the then NY Titans' first head coach.
6. Mark Gastineau, Joe Klecko, Marty Lyons, and Abdul Salaam. Salaam was known by his original name, Larry Faulk, as a 1976 rookie.
7. b. Maynard, who was an original Titan and continued with the Jets through 1972, has 627 receptions, 11,732 receiving yards, and 88 TDs. He was inducted into the Hall of Fame in 1987.
8. False. Buddy Ryan was an assistant coach on the Jets' Super Bowl III team but was head coach with the Eagles and Cardinals, not the Jets.
9. Art Powell.
10. Joe Namath in 1967, when he threw for 4,007 yards.
11. True. Barber's two sons played in the NFL. Marion Barber III was a running back for Dallas and Chicago from 2005 to 2011, and Dominique Barber was a Texans safety from 2008 to 2011. All three Barbers played their collegiate football at the University of Minnesota.
12. b. Jones did this on October 18, 2009.

13. Pat Leahy, whose 1,470 points were scored in 18 years (1974–91) with the Jets.
14. b. Ewbank, who piloted the team for 11 seasons, has an overall losing record with the club—73–78–6.
15. Brett Favre.
16. False. Both, however, were born in Germany.
17. Blue and gold. The club has worn these retro jerseys occasionally in recent seasons.
18. Lou Holtz.
19. False. Grantham unretired to play for Florida in the rival WFL in 1974. He had been a Titan/Jet from 1960 to 1972.
20. John. Curley is his middle name.
21. Tom Tupa, who was originally drafted by the Phoenix Cardinals in 1988 and was that club's backup signal caller for several years.
22. c, in 1964.
23. a.
24. Al Dorow, with 26 TDs.
25. Howard Glenn, guard, suffered a broken neck and died shortly after the October 9, 1960, game.
26. Greece. He grew up in the United States, however, and was drafted out of Brigham Young University.
27. Marvin Jones.
28. c.
29. d.
30. Randy Rasmussen.

OAKLAND RAIDERS

1. Who was the 2001 Oakland coach who went on to oppose (and beat) the Raiders in the Super Bowl the next season?

2. Why did Al Davis leave as Oakland's coach and GM before the 1966 season?

3. Which Raider defensive back led the NFL with 13 interceptions in 1980, then had five more picks during the playoffs?
   - a. Mike Davis
   - b. Lester Hayes
   - c. Odis McKinney
   - d. Dwayne O'Steen
   - e. Burgess Owens

4. What Hall of Fame receiver spent his entire career (1965–78) with the Raiders?

5. What Oakland QB was named 1982 AFC Coach of the Year for the LA Raiders?

6. Name the erstwhile QB who retired at 48 years old as the Raiders' kicker for several years and set the all-time record with 26 pro seasons?

7. True or False: The father of coach Dennis Allen was an NFL player.

8. Who is the 1985 Heisman-winning running back from Auburn who had an injury-shortened career with the Raiders and also played outfield for the KC Royals and Chicago White Sox?

9. What 1975–83 Raider is in the Pro Football Hall of Fame as a linebacker but in the College Hall of Fame as a defensive end? (Hint: He was known as the Mad Stork.)

10. Name the Hall of Fame cornerback acquired from Denver who roamed the Raiders secondary from 1967 to 1978?

11. How did the Raiders acquire Rocket Ismail, Notre Dame receiver?

12. What defensive end starred for the Raiders for 13 years, both in Oakland and in Los Angeles, and has been a popular TV football analyst for many years?

13. Name the Oakland center (uniform number 00) who was named first-team All-AFL during each year of that league's existence, so naturally he's on the All-Time AFL team as presented by the Pro Football Hall of Fame.

14. Who is the Oakland coach from 1969 to 1978 better known for his many decades as a football broadcaster?

15. Which Raider lineman, who lined up against his KC Chief brother twice a year, became the head of the NFL Players Association for many years after he retired?

16. Who won the 1974 NFL MVP and led the team to victory over Minnesota in Super Bowl XI? (Hint: This Alabama Crimson Tide alum was known as the Snake in those days.)

17. Name the assistant who was elevated to head coach during the 1989 season, becoming the NFL's first black head coach in over 60 years?

18. Who was the guard from Penn State voted into eight Pro Bowls who also had a brother in the NFL and a nephew who started at center for the Raiders in 2012?
    a. Max Montoya
    b. Don Mosebar
    c. Todd Peat
    d. Bruce Wilkerson
    e. Steve Wisniewski

19. Match these Raider Hall of Fame stars with their alma mater:

1. Marcus Allen		a.	Arizona State
2. Fred Biletnikoff		b.	Cal Poly San Luis Obispo
3. George Blanda		c.	Florida State
4. Willie Brown		d.	Grambling
5. Dave Casper		e.	Kentucky
6. Al Davis		f.	Miami
7. Mike Haynes		g.	Notre Dame
8. Howie Long		h.	Texas A&I
9. John Madden		i.	USC
10. Jim Otto		j.	Villanova
11. Gene Upshaw		k.	Wittenberg

20. What is Rocket Ismail's real first name?

a. George
b. Isham
c. Jamal
d. Raghib
e. Rocco

21. Which one of these all-time greats never played for the "Silver and Black"?

   a. Eric Dickerson
   b. James Lofton
   c. Ronnie Lott
   d. Deion Sanders
   e. Rod Woodson

22. Who did the Raiders trade to Buffalo to get QB Daryle Lamonica in 1967?

23. In what city did the Raiders play their home games in the inaugural 1960 season?

24. Who was Oakland's first coach when the AFL kicked off in 1960?

25. What All-Pro cornerback from the nearby University of California won the 2010 NFL Man of the Year award?

26. What recent Oakland coach was the youngest NFL head coach in decades when he was hired at age 31? (Hint: He was an offensive coordinator when his father was a well-known defensive coordinator.)

   a. Tom Cable
   b. Bill Callahan
   c. Hue Jackson
   d. Lane Kiffin

27. Which coach got the AFL Raiders into Super Bowl II and resigned from the team with a winning record in 1968 to take the same job with lowly Buffalo?

   a. Al Davis
   b. Tom Flores
   c. John Madden
   d. John Rauch

28. Who is the recent Oakland coach whose NFL playing career consisted of suiting up twice as a 1987 Indianapolis replacement player without ever playing a down?

   a. Tom Cable
   b. Bill Callahan
   c. Hue Jackson
   d. Lane Kiffin

29. Who was the Raiders' 1991 first-round draft pick QB from USC whose father Marv was a Raider guard for one game in 1965 (as well as the team's strength and conditioning coach later on) and who ruined his NFL career early on with drug and alcohol use?

30. The Raiders had the third overall draft pick in 2013. What did they do with it?

OAKLAND RAIDERS ANSWERS

1. Jon Gruden, who moved to Tampa Bay prior to the 2002 season.
2. He became AFL Commissioner. He replaced Joe Foss, who had retired.
3. b.
4. Fred Biletnikoff.
5. Tom Flores.
6. George Blanda.

7. True. His father, Grady Allen, was a Falcons linebacker from 1968 to 1972.
8. Bo Jackson.
9. Ted Hendricks.
10. Willie Brown.
11. The LA Raiders drafted him in 1991, but he signed with Toronto of the CFL, where he played his first two pro seasons, for a then-record contract. He was released by the Canadian team in 1993 because of financial difficulties with the ownership and signed with Los Angeles, whose rights were still valid. He played for the Raiders for three years, including their return to Oakland in 1995.
12. Howie Long.
13. Jim Otto.
14. John Madden.
15. Gene Upshaw. (His kid brother is defensive lineman Marv Upshaw.)
16. Ken Stabler.
17. Art Shell.
18. e. His brother Leo played for the Colts in both Baltimore and Indianapolis, and nephew Stefen (Leo's son) is currently a Raider.
19. 1. i; 2. c; 3. e; 4. d; 5. g; 6. k; 7. a; 8. j; 9. b; 10. f; 11. h.
20. d.
21. d.
22. QB Tom Flores and WR Art Powell for Lamonica and veteran WR Glenn Bass (who was cut).
23. They actually played across the bay in San Francisco because a stadium hadn't been built in Oakland yet.
24. Eddie Erdelatz, former Navy coach.
25. a. Cable was a tackle.
26. d. Kiffin wore out his welcome in Oakland within two years, then coached the University of Tennessee and USC. His father is Monte Kiffin, the defensive coordinator.
27. d. Rauch didn't fare as well with the Bills (two losing seasons) and later coached the Toronto Argonauts of the CFL from 1973 to 1974.
28. Nnamdi Asomugha.

29. Todd Marinovich. Sadly his arrest record for substance abuse continued long after his football career ended.
30. They traded it to Miami for multiple draft choices and used the first of those to select University of Houston CB D.J. Hayden in the first round (12th overall).

PHILADELPHIA EAGLES

1. Name the two Eagle QBs who were brothers and teammates in 1997?

2. What Hall of Fame wide receiver spent the first seven years of his NFL career (1957–63) with the Eagles?

3. Who was the 1978 NFC Coach of the Year?

4. Who is QB Randall Cunningham's brother?

5. Who was the Eagles QB from 1977 to 1986, known as the Polish Rifle, who led the squad to its first Super Bowl appearance in Super Bowl XV?

6. Who was the first Eagles coach to win NFL championships in 1948 and 1949? (Hint: He played for the Canton Bulldogs prior to the formation of the NFL and was an outfielder for the 1919 World Series champ Cincinnati Reds.)

7. What 1952 22nd-round draft pick was cut by the Detroit Lions and eventually sold to Philadelphia after military service,

spending 1956–66 with the Eagles, first at running back, then wide receiver, and finally tight end?

   a. Dick Bielski
   b. Timmy Brown
   c. Ted Dean
   d. Pete Retzlaff
   e. Bobby Walston

8. Which Eagles coach has won the most games in franchise history?

   a. Bert Bell
   b. Greasy Neale
   c. Andy Reid
   d. Buddy Ryan
   e. Dick Vermeil

9. Who was the first Eagle to lead the NFL in rushing?

   a. Billy Barnes
   b. Timmy Brown
   c. Wilbert Montgomery
   d. Clarence Peaks
   e. Steve Van Buren

10. What end spent his entire career with Philadelphia (1947–55) and is known best for catching the game-winning TD in the 1949 championship game? (Hint: He is now in the Hall of Fame.)

11. True or False: Coach Chip Kelly had NFL experience prior to his four years as University of Oregon head coach (2009–12).

12. Which Eagles player did Mark Wahlberg portray in the 2006 film *Invincible*?

a. Vinny Curry
b. Vince Papale
c. Troy Vincent
d. Vince Young

13. What former 49er coach guided the Eagles to the 1960 NFL championship, the team's first in over a decade?

14. Name the Philadelphia Hall of Fame great who led the NFL in sacks in consecutive years (1987 and 1988) after coming over from the rival USFL?

15. Who founded the Eagles and later became the second NFL commissioner (1946–59)?

16. Match these Philadelphia Hall of Fame greats with their alma mater:

1. Chuck Bednarik   a. Duke
2. Bob "Boomer" Brown   b. Indiana
3. Bill Hewitt   c. LSU
4. Sonny Jurgensen   d. Michigan
5. Tommy McDonald   e. Nebraska
6. Pete Pihos   f. Oklahoma
7. Norm Van Brocklin   g. Oregon
8. Steve Van Buren   h. Penn
9. Reggie White   i. Tennessee

17. Which Eagle QB holds the franchise record for most passing yardage in a game, season, and career?

a. Randall Cunningham
b. Sonny Jurgensen
c. Donovan McNabb
d. Tommy Thompson
e. Michael Vick

18. Name the only Eagle who played on both their 1949 and 1960 NFL championship squads?

19. Which of these Eagles head coaches did not also suit up for the team during his playing days?

   a. Marion Campbell
   b. Ed Khayat
   c. Ray Rhodes
   d. Jerry Williams

20. When did the Eagles have their first winning season?

   a. 1929
   b. 1935
   c. 1943
   d. 1944
   e. 1947

21. Did Philadelphia ever have an NFL team prior to the Eagles?

22. Who is the College Hall of Fame tackle from Penn State who was the captain of the Eagles' championship teams of 1948 and 1949 and whose two brothers were also All-Americans for the Nittany Lions?

   a. Otis Douglas
   b. George Savitsky
   c. Vic Sears
   d. Al Wistert

23. By what nickname was linebacker Clyde Scott (1949–52), a future College Hall of Fame inductee, known?

24. True or False: The Eagles won their first-ever game, on October 15, 1933.

25. Which one of these Hall of Famers never played for the Eagles?

   a. Richard Dent
   b. Mike Ditka
   c. James Lofton
   d. Steve Owen
   e. Jim Ringo

26. Who was the Eagles coach from 1952 to 1955 who went on to coach in the CFL with Hamilton (1956–62) and Montreal (1963–65)?

   a. Bud Grant
   b. Wayne Robinson
   c. Jim Trimble
   d. Jerry Williams

27. What linebacker from Georgia Tech played for the Eagles during the first six years (1960–65) of an 11-year NFL career?

   a. Maxie Baughan
   b. Chuck Bednarik
   c. Lee Roy Caffey
   d. Dave Lloyd

28. Who is the early 1980s back whom Dick Vermeil coached while also being his brother-in-law?

   a. Louie Giammona
   b. Vyto Kab
   c. Joe Pisarcik
   d. John Sagnola
   e. Al Vermeil

29. Who was the 1960 US Olympic track team member drafted by the Eagles in 1962 even though he last played football in high school several years before?

    a. Frank Budd
    b. Bob Hayes
    c. Rafer Johnson
    d. Ray Norton
    e. Dave Sime

30. What 2003 Eagles first-round draft pick (15th overall), a defensive end from the Miami Hurricanes, managed only three sacks in three years before injuries ended his NFL career?

PHILADELPHIA EAGLES ANSWERS

1. Older brother Ty Detmer started seven games that year while seventh-round draft pick Koy Detmer spent the season on injured reserve.
2. Tommy McDonald.
3. Dick Vermeil.
4. Sam "Bam" Cunningham is his older brother. Sam played running back for New England from 1973 to 1979 and 1981 to 1982, retiring before Randall got to the NFL.
5. Ron Jaworski.
6. Greasy Neale.
7. d.
8. c. Reid has more wins (140) than the next two coaches combined (Neale and Vermeil). Because he coached the club longer than anyone else, he also has the most losses.
9. e, in 1945. Van Buren also led the league in 1947, 1948, and 1949. No Eagle has ever led the NFL since then.
10. Pete Pihos.
11. False. (Unless you count interviewing for NFL coaching jobs, which Kelly has done several times over the past few years.)
12. b. Papale made the team as a 30-year-old discovered during open tryouts in 1976.
13. Buck Shaw.
14. Reggie White.

15. Bert Bell was co-owner and GM of the Eagles at their 1933 birth. He was a former Penn QB and assistant coach at both Penn and Temple University. His partner, and the team's first coach, was Lud Wray.

16. 1. h; 2. e; 3. d; 4. a; 5. f; 6. b; 7. g; 8. c; 9. i.

17. c.

18. Chuck Bednarik, who played both ways at center and linebacker.

19. c.

20. d. They were 7–1–2 in 1944, good for second place. In 1943 the team was 5–4–1, but it was a merged team with the Steelers known as the Steagles. That team played home games in both Philly and Pittsburgh.

21. Yes, although not called Philadelphia, the Frankford Yellow Jackets played in the NFL from 1924 to 1931, winning the 1926 league championship. (Frankford is a neighborhood in Philadelphia that was absorbed by the city in 1854.) The year 1926 also saw the Philadelphia Quakers take the championship of the AFL, a one-year rival league to the NFL. That AFL and the Quakers went out of business after the season.

22. d.

23. Smackover.

24. False. They lost 56–0 to the New York Giants. However, they ended their first NFL season with a record of three wins, five losses, and one tie—a decent showing for an expansion team.

25. d. Owen, the longtime Giants coach, was an Eagle assistant coach in 1956 and 1957.

26. c.

27. a.

28. a. Al Vermeil, the team's strength and conditioning coach during those years, is Dick's younger brother.

29. a. Budd failed to medal in either of his events, the 100-meter race or the 100-meter relay. He was on the track team at Villanova University (in Philadelphia) but never went out for football there. Budd had a short but mediocre NFL career with the Eagles and Redskins.

30. Jerome McDougle.

PITTSBURGH STEELERS

1. Who were the four members of the Pittsburgh Steel Curtain defensive front during the club's dynasty of the 1970s?

2. Name the Steelers' seven-time Pro Bowl safety known for his long, flowing hair.

3. What recently elected Hall of Fame center played his entire career with the Steelers?

4. Well-known football analyst and sometime actor Terry Bradshaw was the Steelers QB for their first four Super Bowl triumphs in the 1970s. Who were the two QBs he rotated with in his first few seasons before he finally won the job outright?

   a. Joe Gilliam
   b. Terry Hanratty
   c. Bob Leahy
   d. Kent Nix
   e. Dick Shiner

5. Name the Hall of Fame linebacker from Penn State who was the 1975 NFL Defensive Player of the Year.

6. True or False: Coach Chuck Noll played in the NFL.

7. Who is the defensive back enshrined in the Hall of Fame in 2009 who spent the first ten of his 17 NFL seasons in Pittsburgh?

8. What player who played the bulk of his career in Pittsburgh ranks number two on the NFL's all-time scoring list?

9. Which Steeler has gained the most rushing yardage in Super Bowl games?

10. Who is the Hall of Fame cornerback who played 14 years for Pittsburgh (1970–83) and is the franchise's lifetime interceptions leader?

11. What Steeler defensive tackle won the 1969 NFL Defensive Rookie of the Year award despite the team's putrid 1–13 record?

12. Who was named the MVP when the Steelers won Super Bowl XLIII?

  a. Jerome Bettis
  b. Santonio Holmes
  c. Jeff Reed
  d. Ben Roethlisberger
  e. Hines Ward

13. Which Steeler back gained the most yards rushing in a season?

  a. Jerome Bettis
  b. Barry Foster
  c. Franco Harris
  d. Earnest Jackson
  e. Willie Parker

14. Who was the Steelers' placekicker during most of the 1970s?

    a. Gary Anderson

    b. Matt Bahr

    c. Roy Gerela

    d. Gene Mingo

    e. Mark Moseley

15. Match these Pittsburgh NFLers with their nickname:

    1. Jerome Bettis   **a.** Big Daddy

    2. Robert Bleier   **b.** The Bomb

    3. Albert DiMeolo   **c.** Buddy

    4. Forrest Douds   **d.** The Bus

    5. Charles Greene   **e.** Jap

    6. Gene Lipscomb   **f.** Luby

    7. Raymond Parker   **g.** Mean Joe

    8. Tom Tracy   **h.** Rocky

16. Which Steeler QB holds the franchise record of 32 passing touchdowns in a season?

    a. Terry Bradshaw

    b. Bobby Layne

    c. Mark Malone

    d. Ben Roethlisberger

17. Who was Pittsburgh's first-round draft pick in 2013?

18. What Hall of Fame back led the NFL in rushing in 1942 as a rookie and did it again in 1946 despite missing over two years serving in World War II?

    a. Johnny Clement

    b. Bullet Bill Dudley

    c. Tommy Thompson

    d. Andy Tomasic

19. Where was Pittsburgh Hall of Fame defensive tackle (1950–63) Ernie Stautner born?

   a. Boston
   b. Canada
   c. Dallas
   d. Germany
   e. Pittsburgh

20. Who is the Steelers center whose twin brother plays center for the Dolphins?

21. Name the two Hall of Fame wideouts for the Steelers' 1970s and early 1980s teams.

22. Which College Hall of Fame coach, born in Scotland and former coach of Brooklyn (NFL, 1940–41), coached the Steelers in 1946 and 1947?

   a. Joe Bach
   b. Jim Leonard
   c. John McNally
   d. Jock Sutherland

23. Name the 1941 Steelers coach who also coached Duquesne University simultaneously until NFL Commissioner Elmer Layden intervened, insisting he choose one job or the other.

   a. Bert Bell
   b. Johnny Blood
   c. Buff Donnelli
   d. Walt Kiesling

24. What 1989 Steeler draft pick hadn't played college football but had been the NCAA heavyweight-wrestling champion several times?

a. Chris Asbeck
b. Carlton Haselrig
c. Carnel Lake
d. Tom Ricketts
e. Tim Worley

25. Due to manpower shortages during World War II, the Steelers combined with other NFL teams in both 1943 and 1944. Which teams did they merge with in those years?

26. Which Pittsburgh coach had two stints at the club's helm, with 15 years in between?

27. What Notre Dame halfback won the 1953 Heisman Trophy as well as consecutive Maxwell Awards (1952–53), but his NFL career ended after one season with the Steelers because of injury?

a. Lynn Chadnois
b. Jim Finks
c. Johnny Lattner
d. Ray Mathews
e. Fran Rogel

28. True or False: Mike Tomlin's father played in the NFL.

29. What NFL Network draft expert was once the Steelers' tenth-round pick himself as a defensive back in 1981?

30. By what name was the Pittsburgh team known when it entered the NFL in 1933?

PITTSBURGH STEELERS ANSWERS

1. Mean Joe Greene, L.C. Greenwood, Ernie Holmes, and Dwight White.

2. Troy Polamalu.
3. Dermontti Dawson (1988–2000).
4. a and b.
5. Jack Ham.
6. True. He was a Cleveland guard and linebacker from 1953 to 1959.
7. Rod Woodson.
8. Kicker Gary Anderson, with 2,434 points.
9. Franco Harris.
10. Mel Blount.
11. Mean Joe Greene.
12. b. Holmes caught the game-winning TD with 35 seconds left. (Note: Hines Ward was MVP of Super Bowl XL.)
13. b. Foster set the standard with 1,690 yards in 1992.
14. c. Gerela handled the field goals from 1971 to 1978. Bahr was the kicker on the 1979 championship team.
15. 1. d; 2. h; 3. f; 4. e; 5. g; 6. a; 7. c; 8. b.
16. d. He did this in 2007.
17. Jarvis Jones, Georgia Bulldog linebacker.
18. b.
19. d. Ernie hailed from Bavaria and later coached the Frankfurt Galaxy of the World League (NFL Europe) from 1995 to 1997.
20. Maurkice Pouncy. His twin is Mike Pouncy.
21. John Stallworth and Lynn Swann.
22. d.
23. c. Donnelli picked the college position, and Kiesling took over for the rest of the year and the next one.
24. b. Haselrig, a guard, was the club's 12th-round choice in 1989, spending that season on the taxi squad before seeing game action from 1990 to 1993 and appearing in the 1992 Pro Bowl. He also played for the Jets in 1995 and in more recent years has competed in mixed martial arts competitions.
25. The Philadelphia Eagles in 1943 (known as Phil-Pitt or the Steagles) and the Chicago Cardinals in 1944 (known as Card-Pitt).

26. Joe Bach, who was the coach in 1935–36 and again in 1952–53.
27. c.
28. False. His late father, Ed Tomlin, was drafted by the Baltimore Colts in 1968 but played running back for Montreal of the CFL that season.
29. Mike Mayock, who was cut by Pittsburgh but did play for Toronto in the CFL that season. He caught on as a special teamer with the Giants in 1982 and 1983.
30. They were known as the Pirates, the same as the baseball team, until 1939. The team didn't acquire the Steelers name until 1940.

SAN DIEGO
CHARGERS

1. What receiver, nicknamed Bambi, spent 1962–70 as a Charger on the way to the Hall of Fame?

2. Who won the 1961 AFL Rookie of the Year?
   a. Earl Faison, DE
   b. Luther Hayes, WR
   c. Ernie Ladd, DT
   d. Keith Lincoln, HB

3. Name the bearded QB who was the 1982 NFL Offensive Player of the Year?

4. Name the ten-year Charger linebacker (and member of San Diego's 50th anniversary all-time team) whose dad was a defensive lineman with the Rams, Steelers, and Colts.

5. What was kicker Rolf Benirschke known for after retiring from the NFL?

6. True or False: Darren Flutie, wide receiver in 1988, has a brother who played in the NFL.

7. Who was the Charger QB from 1962–72 who later coached Los Angeles of the rival USFL in 1985?

8. Which college defensive back starred as a San Diego wide receiver from 1976 to 1986?

   a. Gill Byrd
   b. Wes Chandler
   c. Charlie Joiner
   d. Kellen Winslow

9. What Charger tackle during the entire AFL run (1960–69) is on the Pro Football Hall of Fame's All-Time AFL team?

10. What 1972 Heisman Trophy-winning running back from Nebraska and 1973 Charger draftee signed with Montreal of the CFL, where he played for four years before finally signing with San Diego for 1977–78?

   a. Hank Bauer
   b. Johnnie Rodgers
   c. Don Woods
   d. Rickey Young

11. Which Charger great is a running back on the Pro Football Hall of Fame's All-Time AFL team?

   a. Gary Garrison
   b. Keith Lincoln
   c. Paul Lowe
   d. Jacque MacKinnon

12. Which Charger has the single-season NFL scoring record of 186 points?

13. What USC linebacker from Samoa did San Diego select in the first round in 1990?

14. Match these San Diego Hall of Fame inductees with their alma mater:

1.	Lance Alworth	**a.**	Arkansas
2.	Fred Dean	**b.**	Grambling
3.	Dan Fouts	**c.**	Louisiana Tech
4.	Sid Gillman	**d.**	Missouri
5.	Charlie Joiner	**e.**	Ohio State
6.	Ron Mix	**f.**	Oregon
7.	Kellen Winslow	**g.**	USC

15. Name the future US congressman who was the Chargers' starting QB for the first two AFL seasons (1960–61)?

16. Which receiver, drafted in the first round by San Diego in 1978, made All-Pro his first three years before being traded to Green Bay in 1981 because of a contract dispute?

a. Larry Burton
b. John Jefferson
c. Charlie Joiner
d. Bob Klein
e. Kellen Winslow

17. What current Charger holds the franchise career receptions record with 642 (and counting)?

18. Which recent Super Bowl coach started 17 games at QB for San Diego in 1999–2000?

19. Which QB set the team's single-season mark with 34 TD passes?

a. Drew Brees
b. Dan Fouts
c. John Hadl
d. Jack Kemp
e. Philip Rivers

20. What much-publicized Notre Dame captain did San Diego select in the second round of the 2013 draft?

21. True or False: Former Washington Huskies, Colorado, and UCLA coach Rick Neuheisel played for the Chargers.

22. Who did San Diego select with the second overall pick in the first round of the 1998 NFL draft who is considered one of the all-time busts in draft history?

23. Which one of these Hall of Fame players never suited up for the Chargers?

a. Deacon Jones
b. Larry Little
c. John Mackey
d. Deion Sanders
e. Johnny Unitas

24. The only time the Chargers had the first overall choice in the NFL draft was 2004. What player did they select?

25. Which LA Charger led the division winner with 44 catches despite passing away from a diabetic attack on November 26, 1960?

a. Ralph Anderson
b. Trusse Norris
c. Don Norton
d. Royce Womble

26. True or False: Charlie Waller, the Chargers' coach in 1969–70, and Ron Waller, coach for part of 1973, are related.

27. Did Coach Mike McCoy play in the NFL?

28. What Chargers coach won the 1990 College Coach of the Year while at Georgia Tech?

29. What 1964 Outland Trophy defensive lineman from the Tennessee Volunteers was a Charger for seven seasons? (Hint: His son Keith was a 49er linebacker for five years.)

30. Which former San Diego lineman was named the AFL's official artist in 1966 and the official sports artist of the 1984 Olympics?

   a. Ernie Barnes
   b. Ernie Ladd
   c. Ernie Park
   d. Ernie Wright

SAN DIEGO CHARGERS ANSWERS

1. Lance Alworth.
2. a.
3. Dan Fouts.
4. Billy Ray Smith Jr.
5. He replaced Pat Sajak as host of the daytime version of *Wheel of Fortune* in 1989. (Sajak remained as host of the evening version.) Rolf was not retained the next fall when the game show moved to CBS. He was inspirational for playing most of his career (1977–86) despite undergoing colostomy surgery.
6. True. QB Doug Flutie, his Boston College teammate, is his brother. Doug played in the NFL from 1986 to 1989 with the Bears and Patriots, as well as with the Bills, Chargers, and Patriots again from 1998 to 2005. Both Fluties are better known for their exploits in the CFL, where they are each enshrined in the Canadian Football Hall of Fame.
7. John Hadl, whose QB on that USFL club was a young Steve Young.
8. c. When he retired, Joiner was the team's career receptions leader with 586 catches.
9. Ron Mix.

10. b.
11. c.
12. LaDanian Tomlinson in 2006, all on 31 touchdowns.
13. Junior Seau.
14. 1. a; 2. c; 3. f; 4. e; 5. b; 6. g; 7. d.
15. Jack Kemp.
16. b.
17. Antonio Gates.
18. Jim Harbaugh.
19. e. Rivers did this in 2008.
20. Manti Te'o, LB.
21. True. Neuheisel, who had started for two years in the rival USFL, was a 1987 replacement QB for San Diego for three games during the NFL strike, his only NFL game action. He suited up but didn't play for Tampa Bay during the last two games of that same season.
22. Ryan Leaf, who won his first two games as a Charger, was benched several games later, was injured his entire second NFL season, and was released after another weak season in 2000.
23. d.
24. Eli Manning, who was promptly traded to the Giants for the draft rights to Philip Rivers and several other draft picks.
25. a. Sadly, the end died at only 23 years old during that first season.
26. False.
27. No. He was a QB cut in camp by Denver who did spend part of a season on Green Bay's practice squad without seeing any game action. He did, however, play for the Calgary Stampeders of the CFL in 1999, as well as in NFL Europe.
28. Bobby Ross, San Diego's coach from 1992 to 1996.
29. Steve DeLong.
30. a. While playing pro football, Barnes was already known for his paintings of football scenes.

SAN FRANCISCO 49ERS

1. Who made "The Catch" off a TD pass from Joe Montana against Dallas late in the January 1982 NFC championship game at Candlestick Park?

2. True or False: Colin Kaepernick was a rookie when he started at quarterback for San Francisco in Super Bowl XLVII.

3. What 2012 49er played in Super Bowl XLVI during the previous season?

4. Name the two men who both played for SF and later were the team's head coach.

5. True or False: The 49ers have a father-son combination that each coached the club at one time.

6. What SF QB holds the team record for most TD passes in a season?

    a. John Brodie
    b. Jeff Garcia
    c. Joe Montana
    d. Y.A. Tittle
    e. Steve Young

7. Which Hall of Fame SF cornerback has a brother who was an Olympic gold medal winner?

8. True or False: The 49ers played an all-initials offensive backfield in the late 1950s or early 1960s.

9. True or False: The 49ers franchise began play in 1950.

10. How did San Francisco fare in 1982 after winning its first championship in Super Bowl XVI?

11. True or False: The 49ers' first-round draft choices in the franchise's first three years in the NFL all wound up in the Hall of Fame.

12. What is San Francisco's record in Super Bowl games?

13. Who holds the NFL record for most career touchdowns?

14. Which SF Hall of Famer was born in Italy?

15. Which 49er has the NFL record for catching TD passes in consecutive games?

    a. Dwight Clark
    b. Randy Moss
    c. Terrell Owens
    d. Jerry Rice
    e. Billy Wilson

16. What trio of 49ers were inducted into the Pro Football Hall of Fame in 2000? (Hint: Two were teammates for many years, one on offense, and the other on defense. The other San Francisco great was a linebacker in the 1960s and 1970s, earlier than the other two.)

17. Which SF offensive tackle was the mayor of Daly City, California, while he was a player?

18. Who was San Francisco's coach for their first three Super Bowl triumphs?

19. Which 49er holds the club record for career sacks?
    a. Hardy Brown
    b. Fred Dean
    c. Cedrick Hardman
    d. Dave Wilcox
    e. Bryant Young

20. What former UCLA lineman started at guard for San Francisco in Super Bowls XVI and XIX, and at center in his final NFL game in Super Bowl XXIII?

21. Who holds the NFL record for most touchdowns in a playoff game?

22. Jeff Garcia became the 49ers' QB following an injury to Steve Young in 1999. Where did Garcia play in 1998?
    a. Browns
    b. Calgary (CFL)
    c. Eagles
    d. Lions
    e. Raiders

23. Which longtime SF star was not on the 1957 team that lost to Detroit in the Western Conference playoff game?

a. Bruce Bosley, G
b. John Brodie, QB
c. Matt Hazeltine, LB
d. Billy Wilson, E
e. Abe Woodson, CB

24. Who was the 49ers' original coach?

a. Frankie Albert
b. Red Hickey
c. Tony Morabito
d. Buck Shaw
e. Red Strader

25. What 1955 halfback went on to a career as an outfielder in major league baseball?

a. Joe Arenas
b. Carroll Hardy
c. Lem Harkey
d. Ernie Smith
e. Norm Standlee

26. Name the two-way back whose lasting fame stems from his college days at Rice when he was running down the sidelines with the ball in the 1954 Cotton Bowl and was tackled by an Alabama player who jumped off the bench to take him down illegally:

a. Gene Babb
b. Larry Barnes
c. Lenny Lyles
d. Dickie Moegle
e. Abe Woodson

27. Who was the 49er tackle whose two sons and three grand-sons also played in the NFL? (Hint: A son and a grandson have the same name he does. The grandson is currently a star linebacker for Green Bay.)

28. Who did the 49ers draft in the first round in 2013?

29. What British-born Olympic athlete earned a tryout with San Francisco in 2013 despite never having played American football on any level?

30. Who was the 49ers' first GM (in the AAFC)?
   a. John Blackinger
   b. Tony Morabito
   c. Allen Sorrell
   d. Lou Spadia
   e. Jack White

SAN FRANCISCO 49ERS ANSWERS

1. Dwight Clark. The leaping catch at the back of the end zone and subsequent extra point gave San Francisco the lead, 28–27. The 49ers had to hold Dallas scoreless for the last drive to win the game. It remains one of the most talked-about moments in NFL history to this day.
2. False. Kaepernick was a second-year player but had been seldom used in his rookie season of 2011. He appeared in three games that year, all started by Alex Smith, completing three passes out of five attempts for a total of 35 yards. His big opportunity came when Smith was injured in midseason in 2012, and he kept the job when Smith was healthy enough to play a few games later. This decision by coach Jim Harbaugh, a former NFL QB himself, was the source of considerable media controversy.
3. Receiver Mario Manningham, who caught five passes for 73 yards for the NY Giants. He came to San Francisco as a free

agent but was injured late in the regular season and was not active for the 2012 playoffs or the Super Bowl, missing the chance to play in the big game two years in a row for different teams.

4. Frankie Albert was QB from 1946 to 1952 and the coach from 1956 to 1958, and Monte Clark was offensive tackle from 1959 to 1961 and coach in 1976.

5. True. Dick Nolan was coach from 1968 to 1975, and his son, Mike Nolan, held the reins from 2005 to the middle of the 2008 campaign.

6. e. Young tops the team list with 36 TDs in 1998. Tittle also had 36 in a year, but that was as a member of the NY Giants.

7. Jimmy Johnson. His older brother, Rafer, was the 1960 decathlon champ for the United States. Rafer Johnson was the presenter when Jimmy was inducted into the Hall of Fame in 1994.

8. True. In 1959 and 1960, the 49ers sometimes played Y.A. Tittle at QB, R.C. Owens at flanker, J.D. Smith at halfback, and C.R. Roberts at fullback. In truth, Roberts was a sub who had less playing time than Hugh McElhenny and Joe "the Jet" Perry. (Other "initials" backs around that period: Until 1956 they had John Henry Johnson, fullback, who was sometimes known as J.H. Johnson. Johnson was traded to Detroit prior to the 1957 season. In 1961, they were joined by fullback J.W. Lockett, but Tittle had been traded to the NY Giants during the off-season, having lost his job as starting QB to John Brodie in 1960.)

9. False. That was the year they joined the NFL. The team was a member of the rival All-America Football Conference (AAFC) during that league's existence, 1946–49. San Francisco was one of three AAFC clubs (along with Cleveland and the original Baltimore Colts) admitted into the NFL as part of the 1950 merger of the two leagues.

10. They missed the playoffs with a 3–6 record in a strike-shortened season.

11. True. Defensive tackle Leo Nomellini was the 1950 pick. A career 49er from 1950 to 1963, he never missed a game in 14 years and was inducted in 1969. The 1951 selection,

Y.A. Tittle, was not a rookie, but players from the disbanded (original) Baltimore Colts were eligible to be drafted along with college seniors. He was with San Francisco from 1951 to 1960 and was inducted in 1971. Fullback Hugh McElhenny was their top choice in 1952. He played the first nine years of his career with San Francisco and was inducted in 1970.

12. Five wins and one defeat. Their narrow loss to the Ravens in Super Bowl XLVII was their first setback after winning in their first five appearances.

13. Jerry Rice with 208. One hundred and eighty-seven of those were made as a 49er for the team record.

14. Leo Nomellini, who hails from Lucca, Italy. He joined San Francisco after playing for the University of Minnesota.

15. d. Rice caught TDs in 13 consecutive games in 1986–87.

16. QB Joe Montana and CB Ronnie Lott are the teammates. Dave Wilcox was the linebacker.

17. Bob St. Clair. Bob was a 49er from 1953 through 1963 and did double duty as mayor of the Bay Area town from 1958 to 1961. At 6'9", he was the tallest NFL player of his day, and probably America's tallest city mayor at that time.

18. Bill Walsh.

19. e. Young had 89.5 sacks between 1994 and 2007. Dean holds the single-season lead with 17.5 in 1983. Cedrick Hardman unofficially had 120 sacks between 1970 and 1979, but sacks didn't become an NFL statistic until 1982.

20. Randy Cross.

21. Ricky Watters. He had an impressive five rushing TDs against the Giants in 1993.

22. b. He played with the Calgary Stampeders in 1998, leading them to Canada's Grey Cup championship.

23. e. Woodson was a rookie the following season (1958), staying with the club until 1964.

24. d. Shaw was the team's original coach in both the All-America Football Conference and the NFL, from 1946 through 1954. Morabito was the owner—the man who started the franchise.

25. b. Hardy played at the University of Colorado and gave up football after one year in San Francisco to play baseball. He was in the majors from 1958 to 1964 and again in 1967.

When he was with the Red Sox, he often was a late-inning defensive replacement for Ted Williams.

26. d. Moegle, the former All-American, was a 49er for five years, from 1955 to 1959. He was on a breakaway run in that Cotton Bowl game when an overzealous, helmetless Tommy Lewis of the University of Alabama left the sidelines to tackle him in the middle of the play. The referee awarded Moegle and Rice an automatic touchdown, and they went on to win the game. Moegle's 265 yards that day was a Cotton Bowl record for 54 years until eclipsed in 2008.

27. Clay Matthews Sr. Matthews played for San Francisco in 1950 and from 1953 to 1955. His son Clay Jr. was a 19-year NFL linebacker from 1978 to 1996, and his other son Bruce Matthews was a Hall of Fame offensive lineman for the Oilers/Tennessee franchise. Grandson Clay III is the Green Bay star whose brother Casey Matthews is currently a linebacker for the Eagles. Another grandson, Kevin Matthews, Bruce's son, is currently a center for the Titans.

28. Eric Reid, LSU safety.

29. Lawrence Okoye, who competed for the UK in the discus throw at the 2012 Olympics and has played rugby in the past. He did participate in the 2013 NFL (predraft) combines but went undrafted.

30. a. Morabito, the owner, hired Blackinger, a friend of his. Blackinger, the GM in 1946 and 1947, didn't have a football background.

SEATTLE SEAHAWKS

1. Name the 2012 Hall of Fame inductee who played his entire 11-year NFL career with Seattle.

2. What all-time Seahawk great served in the U.S. Congress as an Oklahoma Republican from 1994 to 2002?

3. What non-drafted free agent QB was a backup for three and a half years before earning the starting job and still holds the team record for TD passes?

4. Who was the first Seattle coach to win a playoff game?
   a. Dennis Erickson
   b. Tom Flores
   c. Chuck Knox
   d. Jack Patera

5. Name the 2012 rookie quarterback who led Seattle to its first winning record since 2007?

6. Who are the only two Seahawks to win NFL Defensive Player of the Year?

    a. Dave Brown
    b. Kenny Easley
    c. Cortez Kennedy
    d. Earl Thomas
    e. Manu Tuiasosopo

7. Who was Seattle's starting QB in its 1976 expansion season?

    a. Bill Munson
    b. Steve Myer
    c. Jerry Rhome
    d. Jim Zorn

8. True or False: Jack Patera is the only Seattle coach to win NFL Coach of the Year.

9. How did Seattle obtain Steve Largent, their Hall of Fame receiver, in the 1976 expansion season?

    a. college draft pick
    b. expansion draft pick
    c. trade
    d. waivers

10. What Seahawk was NFL MVP in 2005?

11. Which receiver has the most catches in a season (94) in the team's history?

    a. Bobby Engram
    b. Joey Galloway
    c. Steve Largent
    d. Daryl Turner

12. Which back led Seattle with 1,590 rushing yards in 2012?

13. Who was the Seattle defensive tackle who was their first-round draft pick in 1979 and whose son was a backup quarterback in recent years with the Raiders and Jets? (Hint: This player also has several other relatives who played in the NFL.)

14. Which one of these Hall of Fame players never suited up for the Seahawks?

   a. Carl Eller
   b. Franco Harris
   c. Mike McCormack
   d. Warren Moon
   e. John Randle
   f. Jerry Rice

15. Who is Seattle's career sacks leader (with 97.5)?

   a. Jacob Green
   b. Cortez Kennedy
   c. Rufus Porter
   d. Michael Sinclair
   e. Lofa Tatupu

16. Which Seattle defensive player led the NFL with 16.5 sacks in 1998—still a team record?

   a. Chad Brown
   b. Philip Daniels
   c. Cortez Kennedy
   d. Michael Sinclair
   e. Darrin Smith

17. Which 1987 Seattle rookie from Oklahoma was both the highest-paid player in team history (at that time) and the highest paid NFL rookie that year, despite being banned from playing in the January 1987 Orange Bowl game because of steroid use?

18. What Seahawk led the NFL in punting in 1995?

19. Who was Seattle's first-ever draft pick when the team began in 1976?

20. Which one of these Seahawks did *not* have an NFL brother?

    a. Lyle Blackwood
    b. Brian Blades
    c. Brian Bosworth
    d. Matt Hasselbeck
    e. Terry Jackson
    f. Mike Tice
    g. John Yarno

21. Which rookie first-round draft pick gained 1,449 yards rushing in 1983?

22. Match these Seahawks with their alma mater:

    1. Shaun Alexander   **a.** Alabama
    2. Pete Carroll   **b.** Boston College
    3. Kenny Easley   **c.** California
    4. Matt Hasselbeck   **d.** Cal Poly Pomona
    5. Cortez Kennedy   **e.** Miami
    6. Steve Largent   **f.** Pacific
    7. Marshawn Lynch   **g.** Tulsa
    8. Russell Wilson   **h.** UCLA
    9. Jim Zorn   **i.** Wisconsin

23. What Seattle center from 1976 to 1982 got his pro football start with the Southern California Sun club of the WFL in 1975?

24. True or False: Seattle has switched conferences twice over the franchise's existence.

25. Which of these 1976 NFL veterans did *not* bring a Super Bowl ring with him when he joined the expansion Seahawks?

    a. Dave Brown, DB
    b. Mike Curtis, LB
    c. Norm Evans, T
    d. John McMakin, TE
    e. Bill Munson, QB

26. Who is the owner of the Seahawks?

27. Who was Seattle's first-round pick in 1991 who was also the tallest QB in NFL history at 6'8"? (Hint: His brother led each of baseball's major leagues in home runs twice in his career.)

28. Which Seahawks QB was acquired in a trade with Arizona in 1988 after he held out during his entire rookie season and was the Cardinals' 1987 first-round pick?

    a. Stan Gelbaugh
    b. Gale Gilbert
    c. Bruce Mathison
    d. Kelly Stouffer

29. Which Washington Wizards NBA assistant coach (2012–13) had a tryout at safety with Seattle in 1981?

    a. Gene Banks
    b. Sam Cassell
    c. Don Newman
    d. Don Zierden

30. Who was Seattle's first-round draft choice in 2013?

SEATTLE SEAHAWKS ANSWERS

1. Cortez Kennedy, defensive tackle from 1990 to 2000.
2. Steve Largent.
3. Dave Krieg.
4. c. Knox did so in his first year with the team, 1983.
5. Russell Wilson.
6. b (1984) and c (1992).
7. d.
8. False. Chuck Knox also won that award in 1984. Patera got his in 1978.
9. c. The Houston Oilers drafted Largent in the fourth round of the 1976 NFL college draft. They traded him to Seattle during the preseason for a future (1977) eighth-round pick.
10. Shaun Alexander. He led the league in rushing.
11. a, in 2007.
12. Marshawn Lynch.
13. Manu Tuiasosopo.
14. c. McCormack, however, did coach the team for most of a season in 1982. All of the other greats actually played for Seattle during their careers.
15. a.
16. d.
17. Brian "The Boz" Bosworth. His career fizzled out in less than three years despite the hype from his brazen personality and trash talking in the media. Injuries played a role in his decline. He was the star of a 1991 Hollywood action film, *Stone Cold*, two years after leaving the NFL. His acting career likewise was a short one.
18. Rich Tuten, averaging 45.0 yards per punt.
19. Defensive tackle Steve Niehaus.
20. c. Bosworth's nephew Kyle (not brother) is a recent NFL linebacker. (Glen Blackwood was also a defensive back, mainly with the Colts; Bennie Blades was a Detroit defensive back; Tim Hasselbeck was a backup QB for several teams in recent years; Monte Jackson was a cornerback for nine seasons with the Rams and Raiders; John Tice was also a tight end for ten years; George Yarno was guard for Tampa Bay and the USFL.)

21. Curt Warner.
22. 1. a; 2. f; 3. h; 4. b; 5. e; 6. g; 7. c; 8. i; 9. d.
23. Art Kuehn. The first-year NFL player was drafted by the Redskins in 1975 but signed with the rival WFL instead. Nevertheless, Washington still had his rights, and Seattle made him an expansion-draft selection off of the Redskins' roster.
24. True. They were an NFC West team in 1976 and flip-flopped with Tampa Bay in 1977, moving to the AFC West. In 2002, the Seahawks switched back to the NFC West.
25. e. Munson never played for a Super Bowl winner. Brown was on the 1975 Steelers, Curtis played with the 1970 Baltimore Colts, Evans was on Miami's 1972 and 1973 champions, and McMakin was on the 1974 Steelers. All of this winning experience couldn't help Seattle to a better record than 2–12 that year.
26. Paul Allen, cofounder of the Microsoft Corporation.
27. Dan McGwire, whose brother Mark is currently a coach with the LA Dodgers.
28. d.
29. c. Newman didn't make the club but spent seven years in Canada in the CFL. He also was the head basketball coach at Sacramento State and Arizona State during the 1990s.
30. They didn't have one, trading the choice away previously. They didn't pick until the last choice in the second round when they selected a Texas A&M running back with the unlikely name of Christine Michael. (Yes, he's a man.)

ST. LOUIS RAMS

1. In what city did the Rams originate?

   a. Anaheim
   b. Cleveland
   c. Los Angeles
   d. St. Louis

2. What two receivers were Rams teammates between 1949 and 1956 and are both in the Hall of Fame?

3. Which Ram quarterback holds the NFL single-game record for passing yards?

   a. Roman Gabriel
   b. Norm Van Brocklin
   c. Billy Wade
   d. Kurt Warner

4. True or False: 1970s defensive teammates Jack Youngblood and Jim Youngblood are brothers.

5. Name the defensive linemen that constituted the LA Rams' famed Fearsome Foursome of the 1960s.

6. Rams Hall of Fame quarterback (and coach) Bob Waterfield was married to which famous actress?

   a. Marilyn Monroe
   b. Jane Russell
   c. Lillian Russell
   d. Lana Turner

7. True or False: The Rams are the only team to play a Super Bowl game in their home stadium.

8. How was Kurt Warner, the QB who led St. Louis to its only Super Bowl victory, acquired by the team?

   a. Arena League free agent
   b. on waivers from the Bears
   c. in a trade with the Packers
   d. in a trade with Amsterdam of the World League

9. What player did the Rams select first overall in the 1997 NFL draft?

10. Who was the Rams' GM in 1959? (Hint: The MVP of the Super Bowl gets the trophy named in his honor.)

11. Who established the NFL single-season rushing yardage record while with the 1984 LA Rams?

12. Which LA Ram set an NFL record with two safeties in one game on October 21, 1973, versus Green Bay?

    a. Larry Brooks, DT
    b. Cullen Bryant, S
    c. Fred Dryer, DE
    d. Merlin Olsen, DT
    e. Jack Reynolds, LB

13. Which Hall of Fame guard played his entire 13-year NFL career with the LA Rams?

14. Which LA Rams receiver set the record for NFL reception yards in a game on November 26, 1989, versus New Orleans?

    a. Flipper Anderson
    b. Ron Brown
    c. Henry Ellard
    d. Damone Johnson
    e. Mike Young

15. What Ram QB from 1976–81 broke in with Southern California of the rival WFL, was a Rhodes Scholar before joining Los Angeles, and is now the athletic director at USC?

16. What Hall of Fame defensive back set the NFL single-season interception record as a rookie? (Hint: The Rams traded him to the Cardinals two years later.)

17. Vince Ferragamo was a Rams QB from 1977 to 1984 with the exception of 1981. Why didn't he play for the team that year?

18. Did 1950s head coach Sid Gillman ever play for the team?

19. True or False: Keith Lyle, safety in both Los Angeles and St. Louis, followed in his father's footsteps by playing the same position in the NFL.

20. What Rams head coach is also the only NFL coach to manage a major league baseball team?

21. Who bought the Rams from the estate of the late Dan F. Reeves in 1972?

22. Name the 1972 14th-round draft pick who spent his entire NFL career with the team and went to five Pro Bowls? (Hint: He later became an assistant coach with the club.)

23. What brothers led the Cleveland Rams to their first NFL championship in 1945? (Hint: They both played for Knute Rockne at Notre Dame in the 1920s.)

24. Why didn't the Rams field a team in the NFL in 1943?

25. Which member of the Pro Football Hall of Fame's 1963 first induction class was the Cleveland Rams' coach from 1939 to 1942?

26. What 1973 Heisman winner from Penn State was the Rams' first-round draft pick in 1974?

27. What Oregon State QB was the 1962 Heisman Trophy and Maxwell Award winner drafted first overall by Los Angeles in 1963 and is considered a bust as a pro?

28. Which Nebraska running back was selected sixth overall by the Rams in 1996 but never panned out because of frequent arrests and his refusal to attend practices?

29. Who were the Rams' two first-round draft choices in 2013?

30. True or False: The Rams are the first NFL team to have a design (other than a center stripe) on their helmets.

ST. LOUIS RAMS ANSWERS

1. b. The Rams started in Cleveland in the AFL, a rival league in 1936. They joined the NFL the next year. After winning the 1945 NFL championship in Cleveland, the Rams moved to Los Angeles in 1946 and on to St. Louis in 1995.
2. Crazy Legs Hirsch and Tom Fears.
3. b. Van Brocklin threw for 554 yards for Los Angeles on September 28, 1951.
4. False. They're not related.
5. Rosey Grier, Deacon Jones, Lamar Lundy, and Merlin Olsen. Jones and Olsen are inductees in the Hall of Fame in Canton.
6. b. Russell and Waterfield were married during his entire NFL playing and coaching career.
7. False. The LA Rams lost to Pittsburgh in Super Bowl XIV, which was played in the Rose Bowl in Pasadena in front of the largest crowd in NFL history (103,985). That was not the Rams' home stadium (which was the Los Angeles Coliseum). It was the only time a team has played in a Super Bowl in basically its home city.
8. a. He was signed as a free agent after playing with Iowa (Arena League) in 1998 and assigned by the Rams to Amsterdam (in the developmental World League) for the 1998 spring season and made the Rams squad as third-string QB in the 1998 NFL campaign, getting very limited playing time. He had been cut in training camp by Green Bay and the Bears in previous years. He became St. Louis's starting QB in mid-1999, leading the team to victory over Tennessee in Super Bowl XXXIV at the end of the season.
9. Orlando Pace. Pace was the 1996 Outland Trophy winner for best college lineman. The tackle earned that distinction while playing for Ohio State before joining St. Louis.
10. Pete Rozelle, who left the team to become NFL Commissioner.
11. Eric Dickerson with 2,105 yards.
12. c.
13. Tom Mack (1966–78).

14. a. Anderson scorched the Saints for 336 yards.
15. Pat Haden.
16. Dick "Night Train" Lane with 14 in 1952.
17. He played out his option and signed with Toronto of the CFL. He returned to Los Angeles after his one year in Canada.
18. Yes. He played line for the team in the AFL in 1936, his only pro playing experience.
19. True. His father, Garry Lyle, was a safety for the Bears from 1967 to 1974.
20. Hugo Bezdek. The Rams' first coach in the NFL in 1937 and 1938, he had previously managed the Pittsburgh Pirates. He had coached a few major college football teams.
21. Bob Irsay, who immediately swapped franchises with Baltimore owner Carroll Rosenbloom. The Irsay family has owned the Colts franchise ever since.
22. Larry Brooks, DT.
23. GM Chile Walsh hired his brother Adam Walsh as coach, and they succeeded in taking the franchise to a championship before it moved to Los Angeles for 1946.
24. They suspended operations because owner Dan F. Reeves was serving in the armed forces during World War II.
25. Dutch Clark.
26. John Cappelletti.
27. Terry Baker.
28. Lawrence Phillips.
29. West Virginia receiver Tavon Austin and Georgia LB Alec Ogletree.
30. True. Fred Gehrke, with the club since the Cleveland days, painted the horns on his helmet in 1948 when they were in Los Angeles. Gehrke became Denver's GM decades later in 1977.

TAMPA BAY
BUCCANEERS

1. Which players did Tampa Bay select first overall in the 1986 and 1987 NFL drafts?

2. What Tampa Bay defensive tackle and current *Inside the NFL* and NFL Network football analyst was elected to the Pro Football Hall of Fame in 2013?

3. Who was the first coach in the franchise's history?

4. Name the 1976–80 Buccaneers defensive teammates who were brothers.

5. Who was the first-overall NFL draft pick in 1977? (Hint: He was drafted by his original college coach, and his brother was a well-known R&B singer.)

6. Which Bucs rookie runner gained 1,007 yards in 2010, the highest total for an NFL rookie that year?

7. Which running back was the 2005 NFL Offensive Rookie of the Year?

8. Which Tampa Bay back set a franchise record with 219 rushing yards in a game and set the team record with 1,544 yards in a season a year later?

   a. Mike Alstott
   b. LeGarrette Blount
   c. Warrick Dunn
   d. Earnest Graham
   e. James Wilder

9. Which Bucs QB was the team's first-round draft choice in 1978 and was the first to start for a Bucs playoff team? (Hint: He left the club after five years following a contract dispute, jumping to the rival USFL.)

10. Who was the 1997 AP NFL Offensive Rookie of the Year?

11. Which Buccaneer is a third-generation NFL player?

    a. Ronde Barber, CB
    b. Brian Griese, QB
    c. J.K. McKay, WR
    d. Jim Pyne, OL
    e. Lee Roy Selmon, DE

12. Which Buccaneer had three consecutive seasons of more than 1,000 reception yards from 2005 to 2007?

    a. Antonio Bryant
    b. Michael Clayton
    c. Joey Galloway
    d. Ike Hilliard
    e. Alex Smith

13. Which Tampa Bay player led the team with 1,248 reception yards in 2008?

    a. Arrelious Benn

    b. Antonio Bryant

    c. Earnest Graham

    d. Vincent Jackson

    e. Sammie Stroughter

14. Which QB is the franchise leader in career TDs and passing yardage?

    a. Steve DeBerg

    b. Josh Freeman

    c. Brad Johnson

    d. Vinny Testaverde

    e. Doug Williams

15. How many games did Tampa Bay win in its 1976 expansion season?

16. True or False: Josh Freeman's father also saw game action as an NFL player.

17. Which one of these Bucs defensive stars never won the AP NFL Defensive Player of the Year award?

    a. Derrick Brooks

    b. Simeon Rice

    c. Warren Sapp

    d. Lee Roy Selmon

18. Which Tampa Bay coach has the highest winning percentage in his tenure with the team?

    a. Tony Dungy
    b. Jon Gruden
    c. John McKay
    d. Greg Schiano
    e. Sam Wyche

19. Match these Buccaneers with their alma mater:

1. Ronde Barber	**a.** Auburn
2. LeGarrette Blount	**b.** Boston College
3. Warrick Dunn	**c.** Bucknell
4. Josh Freeman	**d.** Florida State
5. Kevin House	**e.** Kansas State
6. Warren Sapp	**f.** Miami
7. Greg Schiano	**g.** Missouri
8. Lee Roy Selmon	**h.** Oklahoma
9. Jeremy Trueblood	**i.** Oregon
10. James Wilder	**j.** Southern Illinois
11. Cadillac Williams	**k.** Virginia

20. True or False: John Lynch, the Bucs' Pro Bowl safety, had a father who also played in the NFL.

21. Who was Tampa Bay's QB in their Super Bowl XXXVII triumph?

    a. Trent Dilfer
    b. Brian Griese
    c. Brad Johnson
    d. Shaun King
    e. Chris Simms

22. Name the Argentine kicker who was Tampa Bay's third-round draft choice in 1999 and played for the club for five years, including their Super Bowl XXXVII squad. He is the franchise's all-time scoring leader.

23. What linebacker was named to five Pro Bowls in his seven years on the team (1993–99) and was a Tampa Bay radio announcer in 2006 and 2007?

a. Derrick Brooks
b. Jamie Duncan
c. Marcus Jones
d. Keith McCants
e. Hardy Nickerson

24. Which one of these NFL head coaches did *not* spend time as a Tampa Bay assistant coach?

a. Herm Edwards
b. Joe Gibbs
c. David Shula
d. Lovie Smith
e. Mike Tomlin

25. Who was the Buccaneers' starting QB in their 1976 expansion season? (Hint: He won the Heisman Trophy and is a current college coach.)

26. Who was the 1980 Lombardi Award winner and three-time consensus All-American defensive end from Pitt whom Tampa Bay converted to linebacker as a rookie in 1981?

27. Who was the 1978 Maxwell Award–winning QB from Penn State who was a backup for three years with the Bucs before jumping to the rival USFL, where he led the Stars franchise to league championships in 1984 and 1985?

a. Steve DeBerg
b. Chuck Fusina
c. Jerry Golsteyn
d. Jack Thompson
e. Doug Williams

28. What current head coach of the CFL Toronto Argonauts was a backup QB for the Buccaneers from 1996 to 1999?

29. Where was cornerback Aqib Talib born?

    a. Afghanistan
    b. Cleveland
    c. Kansas
    d. Texas
    e. Uzbekistan

30. True or False: WR Ed Gant is the brother of 17-year major league second baseman and outfielder Ron Gant.

TAMPA BAY BUCCANEERS ANSWERS

1. Bo Jackson, Auburn running back (1986), and Vinny Testaverde, University of Miami QB (1987).
2. Warren Sapp.
3. John McKay. The USC College Hall of Fame coaching legend was Tampa Bay's coach from 1976 to 1984.
4. Lee Roy Selmon, DE, and Dewey Selmon, LB-DT, played together for the Buccaneers' first five years of competition. Their older brother, Lucious Selmon, a Patriots draft pick in 1974, spent two seasons with Memphis in the rival WFL, 1974–75.
5. Ricky Bell, drafted by John McKay, his old USC coach. Bell's brother is Archie Bell of Archie Bell and the Drells (of "Tighten Up" fame).
6. LeGarrette Blount.
7. Carnell "Cadillac" Williams.
8. e, in 1983 and 1984.
9. Doug Williams.
10. Warrick Dunn.
11. d. Pyne, who played for Tampa Bay from 1995 to 1997, is the son of George Pyne (Boston Patriots tackle in 1965) and the grandson of George Pyne (tackle on the 1931 Providence Steamrollers). Barber and Selmon have NFL

brothers, Griese's father was a QB, and McKay's father was his coach with the Bucs.

12. c.

13. b.

14. d.

15. Zero. They were a dismal 0–14. They still hold the unwanted distinction as the worst expansion team ever, but the 2008 Lions surpassed them for the worst record by going 0–16 (longer season).

16. False. His father Ron was cut by Kansas City and Buffalo but did spend two years as a linebacker in the USFL with Pittsburgh and Orlando.

17. b. Selmon won in 1979, Sapp in 1999, and Brooks in 2002.

18. a, .549. Gruden, who is second at .512, has the most wins, 60, to Dungy's 56.

19. 1. k; 2. i; 3. d; 4. e; 5. j; 6. f; 7. c; 8. h; 9. b; 10. g; 11. a.

20. False. Almost, however. His father, also John Lynch, was a Drake University linebacker drafted 13th by the Steelers in 1969. He was injured during exhibition games and never saw regular-season action.

21. c.

22. Martin Grammatica.

23. e.

24. c. His brother Mike was once the Bucs' offensive coordinator, however. Mike Shula also was a sub for the team in 1987.

25. Steve Spurrier.

26. Hugh Green.

27. b.

28. Scott Milanovich, whose actual playing time consisted of a mere single game in 1996.

29. b. The defensive back with the foreign-sounding name was born in Ohio's largest city and grew up in Texas. He left the club for New England as a free agent in 2013.

30. False, Ron Gant is his cousin.

TENNESSEE TITANS (INCLUDING HOUSTON OILERS)

1. Name the 1999 Titan from the Super Bowl XXXIV squad who holds the NFL single-season record for most regular-season sacks by a rookie.

2. What Houston Oilers Hall of Fame QB holds the franchise career record for passing yards and passing TDs and played 17 NFL seasons (10 with the Oilers), retiring at age 44?

3. What 1995 Heisman-winning running back was named the 1996 *Sporting News* Offensive Rookie of the Year after the team's last year in Houston?

4. Who is the only owner the Titans/Houston Oilers franchise has ever had?

5. Which Titan broke the all-time NFL single-game record with a perfect eight field goals in eight attempts?

6. Name the Hall of Fame offensive lineman and recent Tennessee coach who spent his entire playing career with the Oilers (1982–93), then became an Oilers/Titans assistant coach (1994–2010) before being promoted to head coach in 2011.

7. Which QB set the all-time AFL record with 36 TD passes, which is still the franchise record as well?

8. What Hall of Fame running back from the University of Texas Longhorns led the AFC in rushing while on the Oilers in his first four seasons?

9. Match these Titans and Oilers with their alma mater:

1. Mike Barber		**a.** East Carolina
2. Rob Bironas		**b.** Georgia Southern
3. Ernest Givens		**c.** Louisiana Tech
4. Ken Houston		**d.** Louisville
5. Billy "White Shoes" Johnson		**e.** Michigan State
6. Chris Johnson		**f.** Penn State
7. Derrick Mason		**g.** Prairie View A&M
8. Bruce Matthews		**h.** Santa Clara
9. Mike Munchak		**i.** Texas
10. Dan Pastorini		**j.** Tiffin
11. Nate Washington		**k.** USC
12. Vince Young		**l.** Widener

10. Name the Houston Oiler defensive line stalwart who spent his whole career with the team (1968–83) and is now in the Hall of Fame?

11. Who is the winningest coach in franchise history?

12. In what year did the Houston Oilers move to Nashville?

13. The Oilers had the AFL Coach of the Year in both 1960 and 1961. Who were these two different men?

14. Which Titan surpassed 1,000 receiving yards in four consecutive years?

    a. Drew Bennett

    b. Kenny Britt

    c. Kevin Dyson

    d. Derrick Mason

    e. Nate Washington

15. Which Hall of Fame offensive lineman played his entire career with the franchise in both Houston and Tennessee (1983–2001) and now is an assistant coach with the team? (Hint: He comes from a family of football players.)

16. Which Titan led the NFL in punting average in 1998 (with 47.2 yards per punt)?

    a. Craig Hentrich

    b. Brett Kern

    c. Reggie Robey

    d. Stephen Tulloch

17. Name the Houston receiver who holds the AFL's all-time record with 101 catches in a season.

    a. Ode Burrell

    b. Bill Groman

    c. Charlie Hennigan

    d. Charlie Joiner

    e. Jerry LeVias

18. Which Titan set the NFL record with 2,509 yards from scrimmage (2,006 of those rushing)?

   a. Chris Brown
   b. Eddie George
   c. Travis Henry
   d. Chris Johnson
   e. LenDale White

19. What Oiler with a "colorful" nickname led the NFL in punt return average in 1975 and 1977 and later led the NFC in that category in 1982 for Atlanta? (Hint: He was named to the NFL 75th Anniversary squad as the punt returner and is a member of the College Football Hall of Fame.)

20. Which kicker is the franchise's all-time scoring leader?

   a. Gary Anderson
   b. Rob Bironas
   c. George Blanda
   d. Al Del Greco
   e. Joe Nedney

21. What Hall of Famer coached the AFL Oilers in 1964?

   a. Sammy Baugh
   b. Sid Gillman
   c. Pop Ivy
   d. Bones Taylor

22. True or False: The father of center Kevin Matthews also played for the team.

23. What 1959 Heisman winner became Houston's first star in the AFL and a member of their early AFL championship teams? (Hint: After football, he became a dentist and is a member of the College Football Hall of Fame.)

24. Name the Hall of Fame safety who played the first six years of his career with the Oilers and was traded to the Redskins in 1973 for five players.

25. Which one of these NFL stars never played for the Houston Oilers?

    a. Mike Ditka
    b. John Henry Johnson
    c. Archie Manning
    d. Ken Stabler
    e. George Webster

26. Name the Houston coach for two seasons in the 1980s who had won five straight Grey Cups in Canada and coached in the rival USFL before landing the Oilers job.

27. Who was the Oilers' first draft choice in 1987 (third overall) at running back whose father Walter spent time as an offensive lineman with the club in its AFL days? (Hints: He later became a pro boxer, is now a Green Bay personnel executive, and has a nephew, Ali, who was an NFL linebacker in recent years.)

28. The Titans used their 2013 second-round draft pick on a local player from the University of Tennessee. Who is he?

29. Name the two teammates at Jackson State who were reunited as Houston Oiler defensive starters in the late 1970s and early 1980s. (Hint: One was a linebacker who made seven straight Pro Bowls; the other was a safety.)

30. True or False: Houston Oilers wide receiver Mike Renfro (1978–83) was a second-generation NFLer.

TENNESSEE TITANS ANSWERS

1. Jevon Kearse, defensive end, with 14.5 sacks that year.
2. Warren Moon. He leads the club with 33,685 passing yards and 196 TDs. Moon spent his first six seasons with Edmonton in the CFL, was an Oiler from 1984 to 1993, and stayed in the league through 2000 for a total of 23 pro seasons. He retired at age 44.
3. Eddie George. George came from Ohio State and stayed with Tennessee until 2003.
4. K.S. "Bud" Adams, who founded the team as an original AFL member in 1960. He turned 90 years old in 2013 and passed away on Oct 21, 2013. His family still owns the team.
5. Rob Bironas set the new record on October 21, 2007.
6. Mike Munchak.
7. George Blanda in 1961.
8. Earl Campbell.
9. 1. c; 2. b; 3. d; 4. g; 5. l; 6. a; 7. e; 8. k; 9. f; 10. h; 11. j; 12. i.
10. Elvin Bethea.
11. Jeff Fisher.
12. 1998. They played 1997 as the Tennessee Oilers in Liberty Bowl Stadium in Memphis for one season before moving to Nashville the next year.
13. Lou Rymkus in 1960 and Wally Lemm in 1961, taking over when Rymkus was fired five games into the season.
14. d. Mason did this from 2001 to 2004, then left for Baltimore as a free agent.
15. Bruce Matthews.
16. a.
17. c, in 1964.
18. d, in 2009.
19. Billy "White Shoes" Johnson.
20. d. Del Greco had 1,060 during his ten years with Houston and Tennessee. Bironas will probably pass him soon.
21. a.
22. True. Hall of Famer Bruce Matthews is also the Titans' offensive line coach, so he was recently Kevin's position coach.

23. Billy Cannon.
24. Ken Houston.
25. a. Ditka signed with the Bears, who selected him in the NFL draft the same year that the Oilers used their first-round AFL pick on him.
26. Hugh Campbell, who was hired partially because he had been Warren Moon's coach in the CFL.
27. Alonzo Highsmith.
28. Wide receiver Justin Hunter.
29. Robert Brazile (LB) and Vernon Perry (S).
30. True. His father, the late Ray Renfro, was a Browns receiver from 1952 to 1963.

WASHINGTON
REDSKINS

1. The Redskins were the winners in the highest scoring game in NFL history. Who did they beat, and how many points did the two teams accumulate?

2. How did Washington obtain fullback John Riggins?

3. Which two men mainly associated with the Redskins were part of the Canton Hall of Fame's first induction group in 1963?

4. What were the two NFL teams that Mike Shanahan coached before coming to the Redskins?

5. How many Redskin head coaches are in the Pro Football Hall of Fame?

    a. 2
    b. 3
    c. 4
    d. 6
    e. 7

6. True or False: Robert Griffin III, Heisman-winning QB, was the first overall pick in the 2012 NFL draft.

7. Name the Redskins QB who was the first black signal caller both to play in and win a Super Bowl.

8. When was the first time the team played in the Super Bowl?

9. What longtime Redskin is the NFL all-time leader in most career punt returns?
   a. Brandon Banks
   b. Eddie Brown
   c. Brian Mitchell
   d. Mike Nelms
   e. Johnny Williams

10. What Redskin holds the team record for most career TDs scored?
    a. Larry Brown
    b. Bobby Mitchell
    c. Art Monk
    d. John Riggins
    e. Charley Taylor

11. In what country was punter Sav Rocca born?

12. How did the Redskins acquire QB Joe Theismann?

13. Who is the Redskins' career leader in receptions and receiving yards as well as most catches in a single season?
    a. Bobby Mitchell
    b. Art Monk
    c. Santana Moss
    d. Ricky Sanders
    e. Charley Taylor

14. Name the Hall of Fame cornerback who played his entire 20-year career with the Skins.

15. Who is the only player from the franchise's original 1932 Boston team to later become the Redskins head coach?

16. Which Washington coach holds the franchise record for most coaching victories?

    a. George Allen
    b. Ray Flaherty
    c. Joe Gibbs
    d. Jack Pardee
    e. Norv Turner

17. When did Washington win its first NFL championship?

18. True or False: The Redskins were the last team to integrate.

19. Match these Redskins with their actual first name:

    1. Sam Baker   a. Albert
    2. Dutch Bergman   b. Arthur
    3. Turk Edwards   c. Charles
    4. Sam Huff   d. Christian
    5. Sonny Jurgensen   e. Hugh
    6. Choo-Choo Justice   f. Loris
    7. Rocky McIntosh   g. Robert
    8. Bo Russell   h. Roger
    9. Bones Taylor   i. Torrance

20. True or False: Washington has thrown a league record 99-yard TD pass more times than any other team.

21. How many times does Washington appear on the NFL's list of top ten seasons in home paid attendance?

a. 2
b. 3
c. 6
d. 9
e. 10

22. What was unique about 1933–34 Boston Redskins coach Bill Dietz's heritage?

23. What Redskins tackle for ten seasons (1981–90) won the 1980 Outland Trophy out of the University of Pittsburgh?

24. Who was the franchise's first coach in 1932, when they were the Boston Braves?

25. Which Redskin head coach was a navy admiral?

26. What Redskins coach was George Gipp's roommate at Notre Dame in 1923 and had an older brother who played pre-NFL pro football and had a brief career as a Cleveland Indians second baseman? (Hint: These two Knute Rockne players shared the same nickname.)

27. What Redskins halfback (1939–42 and 1946–48) became the coach during the 1951 season and was fired during preseason in 1952?

a. Herman Ball
b. Turk Edwards
c. Joe Kuharich
d. Dick Todd

28. In what country was Redskins tackle Shar Pourdanesh born?

    a. Azerbaijan
    b. Canada
    c. India
    d. Iran
    e. Taiwan

29. What Auburn defensive star won both the 1988 Outland and Lombardi awards but had an NFL career that was limited to only two seasons with the Skins because of injuries? (Hint: He's currently an assistant coach with the University of Georgia.)

30. Which 1967 Heisman and Maxwell award–winning QB from UCLA retired after two years of being Washington's backup (to Sonny Jurgensen)?

WASHINGTON REDSKINS ANSWERS

1. NY Giants. 113 total points (72–41) on November 27, 1966.
2. He was signed as a free agent in 1976. He had tallied 1,005 yards rushing as a NY Jet in 1975.
3. Sammy Baugh, QB, and owner-founder George Preston Marshall. (Marshall also owned a basketball team, the Washington Palace Five, in the early hoops major-league ABL in the mid-1920s.) Curly Lambeau was part of that first group, too, but was elected based on his decades in Green Bay rather than his two years coaching the Skins at the end of his career.
4. Denver and the LA Raiders.
5. e. Ray Flaherty, Turk Edwards, Curly Lambeau, Otto Graham, Vince Lombardi, George Allen, Joe Gibbs. Edwards and Graham were elected strictly as players.
6. False. Griffin was second overall, picked right behind QB Andrew Luck, who went to Indianapolis. Griffin did, however, edge Luck out for Offensive Rookie of the Year.
7. Doug Williams.

8. Super Bowl VII on January 14, 1973, when they failed to prevent the Miami Dolphins from achieving an undefeated, untied season.

9. c. Mitchell tops the all-time list with 463 punt returns. He also tops the career list with 231 fair catches.

10. e. He had 90.

11. Australia.

12. He was signed in 1974 after spending three years in Canada with the Toronto Argonauts. He was drafted by the Dolphins in 1971 out of Notre Dame but elected to sign with the CFL instead. Nowadays, Theismann is a well-known football broadcaster on TV.

13. b. Monk has 888 career receptions with a high of 106 in 1984 and a total of 12,026 yards.

14. Darrell Green (1983–2002).

15. Turk Edwards, tackle from 1932 to 1940 and coach from 1946 to 1948.

16. c. Gibbs has 171 wins, over a hundred more than the second-winningest coach on the list.

17. In 1937, the franchise's sixth year of existence and second year in Washington.

18. True. Owner G.P. Marshall had been instrumental in pushing for a "gentleman's agreement" among league owners to not hire black players during the Depression years. There had been at least a few blacks in the league from its 1920 inception through 1933, but none appeared on NFL rosters again until 1946. The Redskins didn't integrate until 1962 with future Hall of Famer Bobby Mitchell and three others. Part of the reason Marshall relented was pressure from President John F. Kennedy to hire blacks or lose public funding of the new DC Stadium in the nation's capital.

19. 1. f; 2. b; 3. a; 4. g; 5. d; 6. c; 7. h; 8. i; 9. e.

20. True. They've done it three times out of the league's overall 13 occurrences. No other team has done it more than once. The first time it happened in NFL history was on October 15, 1939, when Redskin Frank Filchock connected with Andy Farkas. The second time saw George Izo passing to Bobby Mitchell on September 15, 1963, and the last

Redskins pair with a 99-yard hookup were Sonny Jurgensen to Gerry Allen, also on September 15, in 1968.

21. d. Prior to the 2012 season, FedEx Field (formerly Jack Kent Cooke Stadium) had all ten of the top ten seasons. Dallas topped the NFL attendance list in 2012 and joined the all-time list at number four. A recent renovation of FedEx Field has reduced the capacity by several thousand seats. Washington still has the number one single-season spot with 711,471 paid for 2007.

22. Lone Star Dietz was hired partially because he was a Native American (Indian) in keeping with the Redskins name. Dietz, who was a college teammate of Jim Thorpe, was also an accomplished college coach at Washington State, Purdue, Louisiana Tech, and Wyoming.

23. Mark May.

24. Lud Wray, who left after one season to become the original coach (and part-owner) of the 1933 Philadelphia Eagles.

25. The 1949 coach was Vice Admiral John "Billick" Whelchel, just retired from the navy, who had been the coach at the U.S. Naval Academy at Annapolis in 1942 and 1943. He resigned in midseason, citing interference from owner George Preston Marshall.

26. Art "Dutch" Bergman, whose brother Al "Dutch" Bergman was the baseball player.

27. d.

28. d. He is the first Iranian-born player in NFL history and lived in Germany before moving to the United States as a child. He played for the University of Nevada.

29. Tracy Rocker.

30. Gary Beban.

HEAD COACHES

1. Which two NFL coaches who opposed each other often between 1931 and 1940 were teammates at the University of Illinois under legendary coach Bob Zuppke?

2. Who was the first offensive coordinator for the 1968 expansion Cincinnati Bengals under Paul Brown who also went on to become a Hall of Fame coach himself?

3. What former San Diego coach, who is currently coach of Oregon State, played for Bear Bryant as an Alabama undergrad?

4. Who is the former LA Rams and San Diego coach whose father managed baseball's Philadelphia Phillies?

5. What 1920 Cleveland player-coach was also the league's initial vice president until he abruptly left the league after only three games? (Hint: He was Knute Rockne's teammate at Notre Dame.)

   a. Norm Barry
   b. Stan Cofall
   c. Gus Dorais
   d. Cap Edwards

6. Which coach succeeded the late Knute Rockne at Notre Dame and later replaced George Halas with the Bears when the latter left for military service in 1942?

7. Who is the recently deceased coach whose résumé includes coaching stops in the rival WFL, USFL, and CFL and at the University of Houston, in addition to heading three NFL clubs? (Hint: He was an NFL linebacker for 15 seasons.)

8. How many future NFL head coaches were either players or assistant coaches on the 1961 Green Bay team, Vince Lombardi's first championship squad?

   a. 4
   b. 5
   c. 7
   d. 9
   e. 11

9. What St. Louis Cardinals coach is enshrined in the College Football Hall of Fame for his 17 years at the helm of the University of Oklahoma? (Hint: He was the Packers' third-round draft pick in 1937 but passed on a football playing career.)

10. How many pairs of fathers and sons have been head coaches in the NFL?

    a. 1
    b. 2
    c. 5
    d. 7
    e. 10

11. What coach had a nine-year NFL coaching career without having a single winning season? (Hint: He had two separate stints with Atlanta, as well as a few seasons with the Eagles.)

12. Which former AFL linebacker got his coaching start as an assistant in the rival WFL and had a 21-year NFL coaching career with Cleveland, Kansas City, Washington, and San Diego? (Hint: Both his brother and his son have made careers for themselves as NFL assistant coaches.)

13. What offensive coordinator for Dallas's 1992 and 1993 back-to-back Super Bowl wins also has had a 15-year NFL head coaching career with Washington, Oakland, and, most recently, San Diego?

14. Which coach won a Rose Bowl with UCLA, took the Eagles to their first Super Bowl (where they lost to the Raiders), won the only Super Bowl in St. Louis Rams history, and won a division with a 13–3 record at Kansas City in 2003?

15. Which Hall of Famer coached the most NFL seasons?

    a. George Halas
    b. Curly Lambeau
    c. Tom Landry
    d. Steve Owen
    e. Don Shula

16. The record for coaching the most NFL franchises is six. Which of these coaches is the record-holder?

    a. LeRoy "Bull" Andrews
    b. Guy Chamberlin
    c. Jimmy Conzelman
    d. Wade Phillips

17. Which former University of Michigan backfield star was the player-coach of the Buffalo All-Americans during the league's formative years (1920–24) and went on to a 25-year career as a referee in the NFL and AAFC?

a. Hinkey Haines
b. Pat Harder
c. Tommy Hughitt
d. Walt Koppisch

18. Which College Hall of Fame coach had three different stints coaching Ivy League Brown and was coach of the 1931 Providence Steam Rollers?

a. Rip Engle
b. John Heisman
c. Fritz Pollard
d. Ed Robinson
e. Wallace Wade

19. What Notre Dame QB for Knute Rockne doubled as coach in 1924 of the Minneapolis Marines and of St. Thomas College (MN)?

a. Norm Barry
b. Joe Brandy
c. Russ Tollefson
d. Rube Ursella

20. Which former NFL safety from Yale, who was also drafted as a shortstop by the baseball St. Louis Cardinals, had only one winning record in ten seasons as an NFL coach?

21. What AAFC commissioner resigned that job to become coach and part owner of that league's Chicago squad in 1948? (Hint: His Notre Dame "Four Horseman" backfield teammate was Elmer Layden, who was NFL commissioner at that same time.)

22. What coach of the Redskins and the Los Angeles Dons (AAFC) played for the legendary Pop Warner at Stanford

before becoming a member of the 1924 US Olympic rugby squad?

23. Match these coaches from yesteryear with their nickname:

1.	Heartley Anderson	a.	Babe
2.	Bruce Bierce	b.	Bud
3.	Brooke Brewer	c.	Budge
4.	Severin Checkaye	d.	Cap
5.	George Clark	e.	Cooney
6.	Howard Edwards	f.	Dutch
7.	Alfred Garrett	g.	Hunk
8.	Oscar Hendrian	h.	Potsy
9.	George Ruetz	i.	Scotty
10.	Nelson Talbott	j.	Untz

24. Early NFL coaches Swede Erickson, Tubby Griffen, and Brick Muller all have the same first name. What is it?

a. Alfred
b. Bertram
c. Harold
d. John
e. Walter

25. Who coached the 1922 Columbus Panhandles after being a league referee in 1921?

a. Herb Dell
b. Tommy Hughitt
c. Ted Nesser
d. Pete Stinchcomb
e. Gus Tebell

26. Who was the coach of the long-defunct Boston Yanks (1944–46) whose brother was the shortstop for Cincinnati in the 1919 World Series?

27. Which one of these coaches piloted three different NFL clubs during a five-year span (1925–29)?

  a. Jack Depler
  b. Benny Friedman
  c. Fats Henry
  d. Dick Rauch

28. Who coached two original (and long-defunct) NFL franchises in 1924 and 1926? (Hint: He was an all-American halfback at Penn State but never played in the NFL.)

  a. Bull Behman
  b. Punk Berryman
  c. George Gibson
  d. Eddie McNeely
  e. Sam Weir

29. Who coached the Chicago Cardinals and Brooklyn Dodgers in the NFL between 1933 and 1936 and later moved west to become coach and owner of the (minor league) Hollywood Bears of the Pacific Coast Football League? (That team provided a pro opportunity for Kenny Washington, a black player who wasn't allowed to play in the NFL until 1946.)

30. What player-coach of the Rock Island Independents (in the NFL in 1924 and in the [first] AFL in 1926) was also a minor league baseball manager of Dubuque in the Mississippi Valley League in 1924–25 (where he was also team owner in 1925) and Oklahoma City of the Western League in 1926?

  a. Johnny Armstrong
  b. Paddy Driscoll
  c. Hinkey Haines
  d. Al Pierotti

HEAD COACHES ANSWERS

1. The Bears' George Halas and Potsy Clark, coach of Portsmouth, the Detroit Lions, and the Brooklyn Dodgers.
2. Bill Walsh.
3. Mike Riley.
4. Tommy Prothro, son of Doc Prothro.
5. b.
6. Hunk Anderson, who was co-coach with Luke Johnsos during Halas's three-and-a-half-year hiatus.
7. Jack Pardee.
8. c. Three were assistants (Bill Austin, Phil Bengtson, and Norb Hecker) and four were players (Tom Bettis, Forrest Gregg, Jim Ringo, and Bart Starr). In addition, Elijah Pitts was acting coach with Buffalo during a Marv Levy hospitalization (without credit in the record books), and Willie Wood coached in the WFL and the CFL.
9. Bud Wilkinson. He didn't do nearly as well in the pros as he did with the Sooners, where he only had 29 losses in those 17 years. He lost 21 games in only two years with the Cardinals.
10. c. They are Bum and Wade Phillips, Don and Dave Shula, Jim Mora Sr. and Jr., Dick and Mike Nolan, and Buddy and Rex Ryan.
11. Marion Campbell.
12. Marty Schottenheimer. His brother is Kurt and his son is Brian.
13. Norv Turner.
14. Dick Vermeil.
15. a. Papa Bear coached the Chicago Bears (and Decatur Staleys) franchise for 40 years. He also owned the franchise for most of that time.
16. d. Wade Phillips. He broke the record of five when he became Houston's interim coach during the 2013 season. He was fired after the season.
17. c.
18. d. Robinson coached at Brown from 1898 to 1901, 1904 to 1907, and 1910 to 1925.
19. b.

20. Dick Jauron, whose only winning season was 2001, when he went an impressive 13–3 with the Bears. He was with Chicago for five years, Detroit for half a year, and Buffalo for almost four years.

21. Sunny Jim Crowley.

22. Dudley DeGroot.

23. 1. g; 2. i; 3. j; 4. e; 5. h; 6. d; 7. c; 8. f; 9. a; 10. b.

24. c.

25. a. Herb Dell was hired as coach by league president Joe Carr, the same man who had hired him as a ref. Dell went back to being a ref in the NFL the following season.

26. Herb Kopf. His brother Larry Kopf was the baseball player.

27. d. Rauch coached Pottsville from 1925 to 1927, the NY Yankees in 1928, and the Boston Bulldogs, the team that bought the Pottsville franchise, in 1929.

28. b. Berryman coached the Frankford Yellow Jackets in 1924, their first NFL season, and the 1926 Brooklyn Lions in their only NFL season.

29. Paul Schissler.

30. a.

PRO FOOTBALL
HALL OF FAME

1. Why is the Hall of Fame located in Canton, Ohio?

2. What former Baltimore Raven tackle from UCLA was admitted to the College Football Hall of Fame in 2012 and the Pro Hall of Fame in 2013?

3. Who is the only man who has been inducted into the Pro Football Hall of Fame and the Baseball Hall of Fame? (Hint: He's also in the College Football Hall of Fame for his gridiron days at Centenary and Geneva.)

4. How many NFL referees have been inducted into the Canton Hall of Fame?

5. Match these Hall of Fame inductees with their actual given name:

1. Dutch Clark   a. Clarence
2. Paddy Driscoll   b. David
3. Bud Grant   c. Earl
4. Cal Hubbard   d. Harry
5. Deacon Jones   e. Hugh
6. Link Lyman   f. John
7. Ace Parker   g. Robert
8. Shorty Ray   h. William Roy

6. The Hall of Fame is located in Canton, Ohio. How many of the inductees played for the legendary Canton Bulldogs (NFL champs in 1922 and 1923)?

7. The Giants and St. Louis Cardinals, two of the NFL's oldest clubs, played in the first Hall of Fame game in August 1962. Who won?

8. Knute Rockne, who supplemented his income playing pro football until 1919, the year before the NFL was formed, was an outspoken opponent of the pro game. How many Hall of Famers played for the legendary coach at Notre Dame?

9. How many Canton Hall of Famers also played major league baseball?

   a. 1
   b. 3
   c. 5
   d. 7
   e. 14

10. Match these football executives immortalized in Canton with their alma mater:

1.	Charley Bidwell	**a.**	Duquesne
2.	Al Davis	**b.**	Georgetown
3.	Jim Finks	**c.**	Loyola–Chicago
4.	George Preston Marshall	**d.**	Michigan
5.	Dan Reeves	**e.**	Randolph-Macon
6.	Dan Rooney	**f.**	San Francisco
7.	Pete Rozelle	**g.**	Syracuse
8.	Tex Schramm	**h.**	Texas
9.	Ralph Wilson	**i.**	Tulsa

11. How many players are in both the Pro Football and College Football Halls of Fame (as of April 2013)?

    a. 17
    b. 35
    c. 59
    d. 108
    e. 124

12. By contrast, how many coaches are in both the pro and college halls, and who are they?

13. Which university boasts the most Canton enshrinees?

    a. Michigan
    b. Notre Dame
    c. Ohio State
    d. Pittsburgh
    e. USC

14. How many NFL commissioners (or league presidents prior to the creation of the commissioner title) are enshrined in Canton?

15. How many men elected to the Hall were involved with the league in its first season, 1920, when it was called the APFA?

16. Name the two father-and-son combinations who are in the Pro Football Hall of Fame.

17. Who is the only player elected to the Hall of Fame to also be elected in the player category to the Canadian Football Hall of Fame?

18. Who is the only other inductee into both the Canton Pro Hall of Fame and the Canadian Football Hall? (Hint: He was named to both halls for his coaching, although he was a player in both leagues as well.)

19. Name the Hall of Fame back who was the 1940 NFL MVP and turned 100 years old in 2012.

20. What three Hall of Fame players only played for teams that are now defunct?

21. Who are the only two inductees in Canton who were never affiliated with an NFL franchise?

22. Who are the only two Hall of Famers never to attend college?

23. Which Hall of Famer was a medical student and intern during most of his NFL career? (Hint: This future MD had two teammates, Bill Osmanski and John Siegal, who became dentists.)

24. True or False: Outfielders George Halas and Babe Ruth were NY Yankee teammates.

25. Which Hall of Fame coach has a son who was governor of Virginia, then a US Senator from that state in recent years? (Hint: The son is a Republican.)

PRO FOOTBALL HALL OF FAME ANSWERS

1. The Hall of Fame is located in Canton because the original two meetings to form the league (then called the American Professional Football Association) took place there in August and September of 1920, at the Hupmobile auto showroom of Ralph Hay, who also owned the Canton Bulldogs, a charter member of the league.

2. Jonathan Ogden.

3. Cal Hubbard. He's in the Cooperstown shrine for his work as a baseball umpire (not a player). By the way, Centenary is in Shreveport, Louisiana, and Geneva College is in Beaver Falls, Pennsylvania, close to Pittsburgh.

4. None. Unlike the baseball, basketball, and hockey halls, there are no on-field officials who are enshrined. About the closest would be longtime NFL supervisor of officials Shorty Ray, who never donned the striped shirt himself, and Mel Hein, who is in based on his merits as a player but was the AFL's head of officiating during the last four years of that league's existence (1966–69). By that time Mel was already in Canton (1963).

5. 1. c; 2. f; 3. d; 4. g; 5. b; 6. h; 7. a; 8. e.

6. Five—Guy Chamberlin, Joe Guyon, Fats Henry, Link Lyman, and Jim Thorpe.

7. Neither team. It ended in a 21–21 tie. Six future inductees played in that game—Larry Wilson for St. Louis and the Giants' Roosevelt Brown, Frank Gifford, Sam Huff, Andy Robustelli, and Y.A. Tittle.

8. Three. They were Johnny Blood (McNally), Curly Lambeau, and George Trafton. None of them played more than a year for the Fighting Irish before dropping out.

9. d. The seven are Red Badgro, Paddy Driscoll, George Halas, Ernie Nevers, Ace Parker, Jim Thorpe, and, the most recent, Deion Sanders.

10. 1. c; 2. g; 3. i; 4. e; 5. b; 6. a; 7. f; 8. h; 9. d.

11. d. No less than 108 have been inducted into both halls. (Too numerous to list all their names.)

12. Just two, Greasy Neale and Sid Gillman. Neale is in the college hall for his work at Muskingum, West Virginia Wes-

leyan, Marietta, Washington & Jefferson, Virginia, and West Virginia. Gillman is in the college shrine for his coaching at Miami of Ohio and the University of Cincinnati.

13. e. The USC Trojans have 11 players: Marcus Allen, Red Badgro, Frank Gifford, Ronnie Lott, Bruce Matthews, Ron Mix, Anthony Munoz, O.J. Simpson, Lynn Swann, Willie Wood, and Ron Yary.

14. Four—Joe Carr, Bert Bell, Pete Rozelle, and 1920 president Jim Thorpe. In addition, Al Davis, Raiders owner/ GM/coach, was the AFL commissioner for a few months in 1966. When the NFL-AFL merger was negotiated, he resigned from his league post in protest.

15. Ten. Nine are players: Fritz Pollard of Akron; Jim Thorpe, Joe Guyon, and Fats Henry of the Canton Bulldogs; Paddy Driscoll of the Chicago Cardinals; and George Halas, Guy Chamberlin, Jimmy Conzelman, and George Trafton of the Decatur Staleys. Owner/GM Joe Carr of the Columbus Panhandles is the other inductee.

16. Tim and Wellington Mara, NY Giants owners, and Art and Dan Rooney, Pittsburgh Steelers owners.

17. Warren Moon, whose six-year career with the Edmonton Eskimos of the CFL, prior to his NFL days, merited his enshrinement in the Canadian hall.

18. Bud Grant. He coached the Winnipeg Blue Bombers to several CFL Grey Cup championships prior to his long coaching career with the Vikings.

19. Ace Parker, who passed away in 2013 at age 101. He was the oldest living NFL player at the time.

20. Ace Parker, Bruiser Kinard, and Fritz Pollard. Parker and Kinard were teammates for a few years with the NFL Brooklyn Dodgers (pre–World War II), although each played for other teams as well. Pollard, an early black player-coach, played for the league's first champion, Akron (1920), as well as Hammond (IN), Milwaukee, and Providence (and several non-NFL pro teams). None of the clubs he played for survived the Depression.

21. Shorty Ray and Ed Sabol. Ray was the NFL supervisor of officials for many years and helped write and codify the

league rules. Sabol was the founder and driving force for NFL Films and made it possible to view all of the past NFL championships and Super Bowls on film or video since 1962. Ed Sabol is 98 years old (at publication date). Note: Some might say that Commissioner Pete Rozelle also falls into this category, but he was an executive with the LA Rams prior to his appointment as head of the league.

22. Joe Carr and Tim Mara. Carr was the league president from 1921 to 1939 and Columbus owner/GM. Most football historians have doubts that the league would have survived its early days without Carr's "smarts." Mara founded the NY Giants in 1925, and his family still owns the team to this day.

23. Dan Fortmann.

24. False. Halas was a Yankee briefly in 1919, the year before Ruth arrived in New York. The Babe was still with the Red Sox that season.

25. George Allen, whose son is George F. Allen, the politician.

2013 SEASON

1. Two quarterbacks tied the NFL record for most TD passes in a game (seven) in 2013. Select the pair:

   a. Tom Brady
   b. Drew Brees
   c. Joe Flacco
   d. Nick Foles
   e. Peyton Manning

2. Name the team that had the NFL's worst record in 2012 but won its first nine games in 2013 before suffering a loss.

3. The Green Bay Packers have been known for stability at the QB position in recent decades, yet in a five-game stretch during the 2013 season, four different men started at QB in successive games. Who was the only one *not* to be a starting signal caller for the Pack in November 2013?

   a. Brett Favre
   b. Matt Flynn
   c. Aaron Rodgers
   d. Scott Tolzien
   e. Seneca Wallace

4. Who set the record for the NFL's longest touchdown, on a 109-yard kickoff return?

   a. Josh Cribbs
   b. Devin Hester
   c. Jacoby Jones
   d. Cordarrelle Patterson
   e. Darren Sproles

5. Name the Canton Hall of Famer who passed away in mid-November and was an NFL coach, GM, and team president but is enshrined as an offensive lineman.

6. Which Raiders defensive back tied the all-time NFL career record for defensive TDs with a fumble recovery that he took all the way against San Diego on October 6? The record of 13 is also held by Darren Sharper and Rod Woodson.

7. Which New England Patriot star missed the 2013 season while being in prison, indicted for murder?

8. True or False: Detroit's Calvin "Megatron" Johnson broke the NFL reception yards record when he amassed 329 yards receiving on October 27, 2013.

9. Which is the only AFC team to surpass 600 (combined) wins in its history? They achieved this with their first 2013 win.

10. Match the NFL star with his new team for 2013:

    1. Anquan Boldin   a. Arizona
    2. Reggie Bush   b. Denver
    3. Willie Colon   c. Detroit
    4. Percy Harvin   d. Kansas City
    5. Rashard Mendenhall   e. New York Jets
    6. Alex Smith   f. San Francisco
    7. Wes Welker   g. Seattle

2013 SEASON ANSWERS

1. d and e.
2. Kansas City Chiefs.
3. a. The media reported that Green Bay was interested in contacting Favre to return from his retirement, but that proved unfounded. Rodgers was injured on November 4, as was Seneca Wallace on November 10.
4. d. The Vikings receiver made history with his return on October 27. No other TD, by kickoff return or any other means, has been as long in 94 years of league competition.
5. Mike McCormack, who was 83 years old.
6. Charles Woodson.
7. Tight end Aaron Hernandez, who was waived by New England when he was arrested prior to the regular season.
8. False, but almost. Willie "Flipper" Anderson of the Rams still holds the record with 336 yards in a single game, but he needed overtime to do it. Johnson has the record with most receiving yards in a regulation game.
9. The Pittsburgh Steelers, a team that ranks fourth on the all-time list (behind Chicago, Green Bay, and the Giants). Of course, the Steelers are the oldest existing team in the AFC, starting out in 1933.
10. 1. f; 2. c; 3. e; 4. g; 5. a; 6. f; 7. b.

SUPER BOWL

1. Name the former Heisman Trophy winner who was the Super Bowl XXXI MVP?

2. Which four teams have never appeared in the Super Bowl?

3. Which quarterback led the Baltimore Ravens to their first Super Bowl victory in 2001?
   a. Tony Banks
   b. Kyle Boller
   c. Trent Dilfer
   d. Vinny Testaverde

4. How many times have the Cardinals appeared in the Super Bowl?

5. Who has the most Super Bowl coaching wins?

6. Who was Buffalo's coach during their NFL-record four consecutive Super Bowl appearances?

7. When was the last time the Redskins won the Super Bowl?

8. Since moving to St. Louis, how many times have the Rams played in the Super Bowl?

    a. 1
    b. 2
    c. 3
    d. 4

9. What player has appeared in the most Super Bowls?

    a. Terry Bradshaw
    b. Tom Brady
    c. Mike Lodish
    d. Preston Pearson

10. What two black head coaches faced off against one another in Super Bowl XLI?

11. Who was the aging Green Bay receiver, no longer a starter, who caught TD receptions of 37 and 13 yards in Super Bowl I?

    a. Carroll Dale
    b. Boyd Dowler
    c. Marv Fleming
    d. Ron Kramer
    e. Max McGee

12. Three of the four players to score three TDs in a Super Bowl game are 49ers. Name at least two of them.

13. Which Raven was named Super Bowl XLVII MVP?

    a. Anquan Boldin
    b. Joe Flacco
    c. Jacoby Jones
    d. Ray Lewis
    e. Ray Rice

ALL-TIME, ALL-TEAM PRO FOOTBALL QUIZ

14. What player started on defense in a Super Bowl and on offense in another Super Bowl a few years later?

15. When Denver played Atlanta in Super Bowl XXXIII, they faced their longtime coach opposing them? Who is he?

   a. Red Miller
   b. Wade Phillips
   c. John Ralston
   d. Dan Reeves
   e. Mike Shanahan

16. How many of the 49ers' Super Bowl XLVII active roster played at colleges in California?

   a. 0
   b. 2
   c. 7
   d. 9
   e. 11

17. Name the two Hall of Fame teammates who hold the career Super Bowl records for most TD passes and most TDs scored.

18. True or False: Bill Belichick has coached in more Super Bowls than anyone else.

19. Who led his team to a win in Super Bowl XXIV as a rookie head coach?

20. In which Super Bowl did one head coach first oppose a coach who had played for him in the NFL?

21. Who is the career Super Bowl rushing leader?

22. Which competitor holds the record for playing on the most Super Bowl winners?

23. Who coached in the Super Bowl and also played in the NBA Finals?

24. Who is the only player to return two interceptions for touchdowns in the same Super Bowl game?

25. Name the only player to appear in the Super Bowl and the World Series.

SUPER BOWL ANSWERS

1. Desmond Howard, kickoff and punt returner for the Pack in that 1997 championship game. He had 244 combined return yards, including a 99-yard TD return against the Patriots, and is the only special teams player named Super Bowl MVP to date.
2. Cleveland Browns, Detroit Lions, Houston Texans, Jacksonville Jaguars. (Cleveland and Detroit have both won NFL championships prior to the first Super Bowl.)
3. c. Banks began the season as the starter, but Dilfer replaced him several games into the campaign.
4. Only once. They lost 27–23 to Pittsburgh in Super Bowl XLIII at Tampa Bay.
5. Chuck Noll. Noll was a perfect 4–0 as Pittsburgh coach, all within a six-year period.
6. Marv Levy. The Bills lost all four games from Super Bowl XXV to XXVIII.
7. Super Bowl XXVI on January 26, 1992, when they beat Buffalo.
8. b. They won Super Bowl XXXIV and lost Super Bowl XXXVI two years later. (They also had lost once as the Los Angeles Rams.)

9. c. Lodish, a defensive tackle played in six games, losing four consecutive games with Buffalo, later winning twice with Denver.

10. Tony Dungy, Indianapolis, and Lovie Smith, Chicago. Dungy's Colts beat Smith's Bears. Dungy thus became the first black coach to win a Super Bowl.

11. e. McGee got to play extensively that day because Dowler had been hurt.

12. Roger Craig did it first in Super Bowl XIX. Jerry Rice did it twice in Super Bowl XXIV, and again in Super Bowl XXIX. Ricky Watters also had three (one rushing, two receiving) in Super Bowl XXIX as San Francisco beat up on San Diego 49–26. Terrell Davis of Denver is the other player to score three times.

13. b. Flacco was selected over several teammates who also deserved consideration in Baltimore's narrow victory over San Francisco.

14. E.J. Holub, Kansas City Chiefs. He was a linebacker in Super Bowl I and the center in Super Bowl IV.

15. d. Atlanta's coach Reeves was the Broncos' coach from 1981 to 1992.

16. a. Surprisingly, no 49er came from a school in the team's home state.

17. Joe Montana (11 TD passes) and Jerry Rice (8 TDs scored).

18. False. Belichick has coached five games, but Don Shula coached six (with the Baltimore Colts and Miami).

19. George Seifert. Seifert piloted the 49ers squad to its second consecutive NFL championship after replacing the retired Bill Walsh.

20. Super Bowl III. Weeb Ewbank of the AFL New York Jets had Don Shula as a defensive back from 1953 to 1956 on the Baltimore Colts. In the January 1969 game, Shula was coaching Baltimore (NFL), having replaced Ewbank there in 1963. The "teacher" beat the "student," as Ewbank's Jets defeated Shula's Colts 16–7.

21. Pittsburgh's Franco Harris gained 354 yards in four games.

22. Charles Haley, defensive lineman, has five Super Bowl rings—two with San Francisco and three with Dallas.

23. Bud Grant coached Minnesota in four Super Bowls and played for the Minneapolis Lakers in the 1950 NBA Finals.
24. Dwight Smith of Tampa Bay picked off two Oakland passes for scores in Super Bowl XXXVII.
25. Deion "Prime Time" Sanders played in Super Bowls with Dallas and San Francisco as well as in the 1992 World Series for the Atlanta Braves against Toronto.